# Shared Commitments To Conservation

*1999 Annual Report of the U. S. Fish and Wildlife Service*

I0450469

# The United States Fish and Wildlife Service

*History and Mission*

As an asset of tremendous environmental, recreational, and economic importance, this nation's fish and wildlife resources represent a vital part of our natural heritage -- one that is facing increasing pressures every day. For this reason, the mission of the U.S. Fish and Wildlife Service (Service) grows more complex and critical every day. As the Service continues to look for new and better ways to conserve, protect, and enhance fish and wildlife and their habitat, its major responsibilities remain focused on migratory birds, endangered species, certain marine mammals, and freshwater and anadromous fish.

### History of the Service

The Service's origins date back to 1871 when Congress established the U.S. Fish Commission to study the decrease in the nation's food fish and recommend ways to reverse the decline. Placed under the Department of Commerce in 1903, it was renamed the Bureau of Fisheries. Meanwhile Congress created an Office of Economic Ornithology in the Department of Agriculture in 1885 to study the food habits and migratory patterns of birds, especially those that had an effect on agriculture. After several more name changes, this office was renamed the Bureau of Biological Survey in 1905.

The Bureaus of Fisheries and Biological Survey were transferred to the Department of the Interior in 1939 and in 1940 were combined and named the Fish and Wildlife Service. Further reorganization came in 1956 when the Fish and Wildlife Act created the United States Fish and Wildlife Service and established within the agency two separate bureaus -- Commercial Fisheries and Sport Fisheries and Wildlife.

The Bureau of Commercial Fisheries was transferred to the Department of Commerce in 1970 and is now known as the National Marine Fisheries Service. The Bureau of Sport Fisheries and Wildlife remained in Interior. In 1974, the "Bureau" name was dropped and the agency is now simply called the U.S. Fish

and Wildlife Service. In 1993, the Service's research activities were transferred to the U.S. Geological Survey.

Today, Service employees number approximately 7,500 individuals located close to fish and wildlife resources throughout the country. Offices and facilities are located in Washington, D.C., seven regional offices, and in nearly 700 field units, including over 500 national wildlife refuges and 67 national fish hatcheries.

### Mission of the Service

"The Service's mission is, working with others, to conserve, protect and enhance fish, wildlife and plants and their habitats for the continuing benefit of the American people."

Since before recorded history, fish and wildlife resources in the United States have been an integral part of human life. We know that the earliest Americans depended on fish and wildlife for both life sustenance and spiritual nourishment. The kinship of aboriginal Americans to these resources is seen today in their religious and cultural activities. The sea

turtle is viewed as the symbol of eternal life with the great creator. Salmon and other anadromous fishes were and still are celebrated as symbols of the renewal of life. Wildlife served as the spiritual connection with ones ancestors and the creator of all life.

When settlers came to America, they found a land teeming with wildlife. Like Native Americans, they depended on the land's rich wildlife heritage for food and clothing. Colonies were located near rivers for commerce and travel and for a rich supply of fish and wildlife for food. The new settlers fully intended that freedom to hunt for food and to secure water for life would be the right of all, regardless of heritage or status. The framers of our Constitution recognized this and placed great emphasis on natural rights and natural laws. Because of the American ideal to respect fish and wildlife as a resource available for the use and enjoyment of all, it is revered as a public trust resource -- a resource deserving the public's attention and participatory guidance. The United States continues to refine the body of case law and statutes governing the stewardship of fish and wildlife resources.

Communities and people throughout the United States have a strong commitment to the fish and wildlife resources today. Many communities realize tremendous economic benefits from tourism and visitors that come specifically to enjoy watching and pursuing fish and wildlife. Hunting and fishing remain strong components of community culture all along the great river systems of the nation. Americans value and respect their natural resource heritage.

The U.S. Fish and Wildlife Service has the privilege of being the primary agency responsible for the protection, conservation, and renewal of these resources for this and future generations. We accept this responsibility and challenge with optimism and resolve to pass along to future generations of stewards a fish and wildlife resource heritage that is as strong or stronger than when it was entrusted to us.

# Message from the Director

One of my top priorities as Director is to improve the way the U.S. Fish and Wildlife Service communicates and works with our public and our partners. It is important that we provide a clear picture of the needs of fish and wildlife resources and the consequences of human intervention - both favorable and unfavorable. Demographers estimate that by the year 2050 the population of the United States will increase by 125 million people, the equivalent of 15 New York Cities. It is inevitable that as we move into the next millenium, competition as well as the need for open spaces will increase. We must find solutions that address both human and wildlife needs. Partnerships, therefore, will play a large part in future conservation efforts, and our work must be understood by the public. In the next century, many of the great conservation successes will be achieved in cooperation with people who have a variety of different perspectives on resource management. We can only reach our conservation goals by understanding others points of views and improving our ability to convey our mission.

We have learned through our increasing number of partnerships that an informed and engaged public can make all the difference. Public and private partners bring fresh ideas, local knowledge, increased resources and dedication to our partnership work. They often allow us to double or triple our conservation efforts, and thus to leverage limited resources. We will continue to create new opportunities for Americans and the global community to share their commitment to conservation through formal and informal partnerships. In this report, the Service highlights partnerships that have enhanced fish and wildlife resources and their management through innovative cooperation. We are building a future for shared commitments to conservation through the partnerships of today.

This Annual Report for Fiscal Year 1999 is part of our outreach and communication effort. It provides a road map of the Service's future direction, an overview of the Service's diverse programs and accomplishments, and an accounting for the funds used by the Service. We expanded the Stewardship and Program Highlights to provide more information on the role of the Service in maintaining healthy environments that fish and wildlife need and how we protect the natural resources in America's conservation units. The Statement of Net Cost in our financial statements provides information on the costs of attaining the performance at the Service's program goal level.

We hope that this report will help you better understand what we do, how much fish and wildlife and plants depend on our shared commitments to conservation, the costs of our efforts, and how much more we can accomplish by working together.

*Jamie Rappaport Clark*

Jamie Rappaport Clark

# Message from the Chief Financial Officer

Over the years, the Service has come to recognize that conservation is a shared concern, one that is deeply rooted in the Service's workforce and seriously regarded by many others as well. As a result, the Service has been able to enter into partnerships that conserve fish and wildlife and their habitat. By emphasizing *shared* commitment to conservation, the Service understands that its role as a leader in natural resource conservation depends on being accountable. The Service's conservation mission encompasses managing an enormous array of assets. These include financial resources exceeding $1 billion as well as substantial property, plant and equipment assets. We take our stewardship responsibilities over these assets very seriously.

In 1999, the Service undertook a number of initiatives to safeguard our assets and improve our reporting capabilities. We began the year by conducting a comprehensive review of all our facilities, communication and data systems in preparation for the Year 2000. As a result of this review, necessary upgrades and corrective actions are being taken and contingency plans have been developed to assure that there will be no significant disruptions at Service facilities. The overall maintenance of Service facilities are a top concern. We continue to move ahead in 1999 with managing our maintenance programs more aggressively. The Service joined other bureaus in the Department of the Interior in emphasizing planning, prioritization and scrutiny of maintenance projects. Through efforts like these, we have come to recognize that the Service needs to improve its management of facilities information. Previously, facilities information has resided in a number of systems which lacked standardized data. To get better facilities information, the Service began efforts to standardize and integrate the information residing in our maintenance, property, contaminant, and financial management systems. The effort will result in merging standardized facilities data from the various facilities systems into a common system call the Facilities Management Information System, or FACMIS. We believe FACMIS will improve the overall completeness and quality of facilities information needed to make sound management decisions.

On a final note, I want to emphasize the importance of the roles played by the Department of the Interior's Office of Inspector General and the General Accounting Office. The Service's financial statements are audited annually by independent auditors of the OIG and GAO. In addition, the Service's program activities are audited periodically by the OIG and GAO. The Service welcomes these reviews and views them as an integral part of our being accountable. We strive continuously to utilize these audits as an opportunity to identify existing weaknesses so that we can improve our management practices. As we increasingly leverage our resources through partnerships, it is likewise increasingly important to verify and communicate that the Service is a well managed, credible and effective organization.

John G. Rogers

USFWS/Dan O'Neal

# Table of Contents

I.      **The United States Fish and Wildlife Service**
        History and Mission ................................................................................................ i
        Message from the Director ...................................................................................... ii
        Message from the Chief Financial Officer ........................................................ iii

II.     **Program Highlights**
        Sustaining Fish and Wildlife Populations ........................................................ 1
        Conserving Habitat .................................................................................................. 10
        Linking Wildlife and People ................................................................................ 16

III.    **Stewardship**
        Stewardship Lands .................................................................................................. 23
                Stewardship Lands and Facilities and Their Locations ................... 23
                Uses of Stewardship Lands ........................................................................ 23
                Revenue from Stewardship Assets .......................................................... 26
                Net Change in Stewardship Land Acreage ........................................... 27
                Condition of Stewardship Lands ............................................................. 28
        Heritage Assets ........................................................................................................ 29
                Condition of Heritage Asset Facilities .................................................. 30
                Cultural Resources ...................................................................................... 30
                Museum Collections ..................................................................................... 31
                Special Designations ................................................................................... 32

IV.     **Financial Statements**
        Overview of Financial Results of Service Operations ................................... 37
        Principal Financial Statements ........................................................................... 40
        Notes to Principal Financial Statements ......................................................... 46
        Independent Auditor's Report .............................................................................. 53

# Program Highlights

*Shared Commitments to Conservation*

Meeting the challenges of providing and protecting a healthy environment for fish and wildlife and for people is central to the programs of the U.S. Fish and Wildlife Service (Service) and is firmly based on tradition since its predecessor agencies were established more than a century ago. Meeting these challenges requires the cooperation and support of other Federal agencies, State and local governments, foreign governments, conservation groups, and local communities. Dedicated Americans, combined with our dedicated International partners, are sharing a common commitment to conservation and are working hand-in-hand with the Service to ensure that our Nation's irreplaceable natural heritage and the world's fish and wildlife resources are protected for the enjoyment of this and future generations.

Portions of this narrative reference specific program accomplishments achieved under the Service's mission or strategic goals identified in its revised 5-Year Strategic Plan. This year the Service selected a subset of specific strategic goals, one for each of the three mission goals, under which to report specific program performance in this report. Another, more comprehensive report on all program achievements under each strategic and mission goal presented in the Service's 5-Year Strategic Plan can be found in the Service's budget documents. The purpose of this report is to highlight general program achievements of the Service, in cooperation with its partners, in a structure that parallels its three mission goals which are: (1) sustaining fish and wildlife populations; (2) conserving habitat; and, (3) linking wildlife and people through fostering public use and enjoyment of fish and wildlife resources. Further, the Service completed its Statement of Net Cost, whereby the Service identifies its expenditures to meet each of the three mission goals. Please refer to both sections, the Message from the Chief Financial Officer and the Financial Statements, for detailed information on how the Service identified these costs and allocated them to each mission goal.

## Sustaining Fish and Wildlife Populations

Many of the Nation's and the world's native fish, wildlife and plant populations are declining or are at historic low levels due to habitat degradation, inadequate fish passage, over-use, poaching, illegal trade in wildlife and wildlife products, introductions of invasive or nonindigenous species, poor land management practices, or urbanization. In partnership with other Federal, State and tribal governments, foreign governments, and a variety of private interests, the Service is effectively contributing to the conservation of fish, wildlife and plants, both nationally and worldwide.

The Service emphasizes proactive species conservation for many species of fish, wildlife and plants through the Candidate Conservation Program. The goal of Candidate Conservation is to prevent listing of species under the Endangered Species Act (ESA). This program takes a collaborative approach with States and Territories, other Federal agencies and the private sector to identify species that need conservation and then cooperatively plan and take actions to conserve those species. Initiating conservation actions early is important because simpler, more cost-effective conservation options can be available and conservation is more likely to be ultimately successful. Also, potential conflicts caused by species listing may be avoided and flexibility for landowners and land managers can be maintained.

Voluntary Candidate Conservation Agreements, CCAs, are established with partners to identify threats to candidate species, plan the measures needed to stabilize and conserve them, implement the measures, and monitor their successes. During this fiscal year, the Service implemented over 70 conservation agreements covering 78 species. As a result, the Service hopes to prevent listing for these species. Many of these agreements successfully removed threats so listing was avoided. Some of the species for which listing was prevented are: three California plants (Cuyamaca Lake Downingia, Parish's meadowfoam, and

## Partnerships That Benefit Threatened and Endangered Species

Tiger Beetle     USFWS/C. Barry Knisley

The Service's Candidate Conservation Program is becoming very popular and the demand for new agreements is on the rise. This program reduces the number of species added to the list of threatened and endangered species and examples include partnerships with the Service that either:

Make Listing Unnecessary -- For the Coral Pink Sand Dunes tiger beetle in Utah through a conservation agreement with Bureau of Land Management and the Utah Division of Parks and Recreation, or

Remove Species from Candidate Listing -- For the Umpqua mariposa lily in Oregon through conservation agreements with the Bureau of Land Management and U.S. Forest Service.

Additionally, there are over 60 species the Service proposed to list under the Endangered Species Act that can benefit from the Candidate Conservation Program in future years.

Umpqua marisposa lily
USFWS/Nancy Fredricks

Cuyamaca larkspur); flat-tailed horned lizard; Arizona bugbane; Jemez Mountain salamander; and, Cassatot leafcup. Monitoring of CCAs ensures that biological goals for the covered species are achieved and that threats to the species are reduced. As the success for this program grows, so does the demand for new agreements.

Great strides have been made in the recovery of listed species with the Service considering the delisting or reclassification of over 20 species, including the peregrine falcon and Aleutian Canada goose, which were delisted in 1999. Other species considered this year include the bald eagle, gray wolf, brown pelican, Columbian white-tailed deer, Tinian monarch, Heliotrope milk-vetch, and Robbin's cinquefoil.

As an integral tool in the Service's overall effort to protect and recover endangered species, law enforcement personnel develop partnerships with conservation groups, State and Federal agencies, and others, to promote greater understanding of the need for endangered species protection and the consequences of violating related Federal and State laws. Special agents assist in habitat conservation planning and play a major role in evaluating and monitoring incidental take permits to ensure

prevent the introduction of invasive species, and additional cooperative enforcement ventures to reduce commercial exploitation.

Law enforcement efforts to protect the Nation's fishery resources target the illegal take and commercialization of native fish stocks. Successful enforcement actions have uncovered a growing, highly profitable, national and international illegal fisheries industry dealing in freshwater mussels, paddlefish, sturgeon, lake trout of the Great Lakes, and other species of concern. Service special agents conduct multi-State investigations to control this growing and highly profitable illegal industry and build on partnerships with State and international enforcement agencies.

The Service's work with external partners to protect and restore fishery resources is exemplified through the Anadromous Fish Management Program. The Service provides scientific expertise and technical assistance to tribes, other Federal agencies, foreign governments, States, and other programs of the Service to develop and implement anadromous fishery management plans. These plans cover such culturally and economically significant species as Pacific and Atlantic salmon, Pacific steelhead trout, American shad, sturgeon, American eel, and striped

Rio Grande Cutthroat Trout                               USFWS/LLoyde Hazzard

compatibility with current laws and permit holder compliance. Other law enforcement efforts that protect and recover endangered species include increased patrols to deter would-be violators, expanded efforts to detect and

bass. Service fishery biologists help with restoring fisheries through identifying and protecting crucial fish habitats; monitoring water quality and quantity; repairing degraded habitats; and providing unhampered fish passage. Service biologists further assess the abundance, recruitment, and limiting factors of wild fish stocks to establish safe harvest limits, evaluate management strategies, and design hatchery products that contribute to species and habitat restoration. The

Manatee                                    USFWS Photo

program works closely with the Service's Endangered Species program and the National Marine Fisheries Service in conducting biological investigations related to the listing and recovery of endangered fish.

Another important fishery resource management program helping our partners is the National Broodstock Program, which was established over 25 years ago to ensure the availability of adequate numbers of disease-free, genetically distinct strains of trout eggs needed to meet the production needs of the National Fish Hatchery System. In FY 1999, broodstock program hatcheries produced millions of trout eggs that were provided to Service hatcheries, State cooperators, other Federal agencies, research institutions, and universities. These eggs were used by the Service and State cooperators to support critical restoration efforts (i.e., stocking of lake trout in the Great Lakes), meet mitigation responsibilities as the result of Federal water development projects, and provide recreational fishing opportunities for the 50 million people who fish annually.

Within its Federal leadership role, the Service maintains desired strains of broodstocks to meet the restoration and mitigation needs of the different aquatic

systems throughout the United States. Currently 22 different strains of trout including rainbow, brown, brook, lake, and cutthroat are available through the National Broodstock Program. The Service continues to receive requests from State cooperators for additional strains

needed to meet specific fishery management needs. Strain Management Plans are being developed for all broodstocks currently held on Service facilities. The plans ensure that all Service broodstocks are properly managed using established guidelines for maintaining genetic integrity.

In addition to freshwater and anadromous species, the Service emphasizes proactive species conservation and protection for marine species. Pursuant to the Marine Mammal Protection Act (MMPA), the Service manages the northern sea otter in Alaska and Washington State, polar bear and Pacific walrus in Alaska, and supports efforts to recover the listed southern sea otter in California and the West Indian manatee in Florida and Puerto Rico. Marine mammal populations are protected and enhanced through enforcement, education, and outreach efforts by Service biologists.

For example, the Service worked closely with Canada this year to obtain information on the management of their polar bear populations. Based on an evaluation of the new data provided and criteria established under the MMPA, the Service approved two additional populations from which polar bears can be sustainably taken under Canada's polar

USFWS Photo

bear management plan. This demonstrates that it is possible to allow sustainable use of a protected species through adequate management planning and effective implementation.

And in South Florida, the Service increased enforcement of speed limits for recreational and commercial boaters operating in manatee zones by organizing multi-agency task forces that target

achieving goal 1.4 for marine mammals includes preparing or reviewing species management plans; implementing the 1994 amendments to the MMPA; preparing, reviewing, and revising stock assessments; and developing and implementing marine mammal incidental take regulations.

The active involvement of our State partners is integral to the Service achieving its species conservation goals.

*It is possible to allow sustainable use of a protected species through adequate management planning and effective implementation.*

Polar Bear                                                          USFWS/Dave Olsen

seasonal high boater use areas. Increased education efforts are on-going to encourage compliance of speed limits, and to heighten public awareness of the manatee's perilous status. In California, Service special agents monitor sea otter/ fisherman interactions in sea otter management zones, and continue to increase efforts to improve cooperation among all interested parties.

Under mission goal 1, Sustaining Fish and Wildlife Populations, and strategic goal 1.4 entitled, "Marine Mammals," the Service set a goal for itself in FY 1999 to provide protection to "100% of marine mammal populations over which the Service has jurisdiction" by ensuring that these populations "will be at sustainable population levels or protected by conservation agreements." The Service fully achieved its goal this year by having in place conservation agreements for all non-listed marine mammal populations of polar bear, walrus, and sea otter in the United States. (Marine mammal protection goals for listed species are reported under the Service's strategic goal 1.2 entitled, "Imperiled Species," which can be found in separate Service budget documents.) The Service's role in

As an example this year, Service biologists, chemists, and law enforcement agents, working closely with the State of Florida and other Federal agencies, identified organochlorine pesticides as the cause of migratory bird mortality in an area north of Lake Apopka in Florida. The quick, coordinated and joint response of the Service and its partners to this emergency situation reduced further losses of endangered wood storks, great blue herons, white pelicans, and other fish-eating birds. Continued joint commitments to remediation and cleanup of the site are providing future habitat for these, and other, migratory birds.

Cooperation among our Federal partners is essential to the Service's success in species conservation. The Environmental Protection Agency registers pesticides and provides guidance for their use under the Federal Insecticide, Fungicide and Rodenticide Act. The Service works with EPA on reviewing the registration of many pesticides. This year the Service provided information to EPA on the impacts of chlofenapyr (Pirate) on endangered species, migratory birds and aquatic resources. Pirate is one of the most reproductively toxic pesticides to birds that the EPA has ever considered for registration. In consideration of the Service's input, the EPA is carefully reconsidering registration of the pesticide and whether it can be used on crops in the United States.

In order to improve existing information on wildlife populations, the Service relies on State wildlife agencies and their cooperation to achieve national surveys. FY 1999 was the first year during which all States except Hawaii participated in the Service's Migratory Bird Harvest Information Program (HIP). This program, initiated in 1992, improves the national waterfowl hunter survey which allows the Service to obtain reliable national harvest estimates for all migratory bird species. We conducted new HIP surveys of all waterfowl, dove, band-tailed pigeon, woodcock, snipe, coot rail, and gallinule hunters in all States. These harvest surveys, conducted annually, contribute significantly to conserving and managing populations of hunted bird species.

enhanced statistical models and high-tech inventory tools to estimate migratory bird abundance. The AMAT and its products will continue to assist the Service and its partners in improving migratory bird management decisions.

To many people, birds represent their only day-to-day contact with the natural world. With environmentally aware citizens, urban communities can play a crucial role in migratory bird conservation. The Urban Treaties for Bird Conservation Program capitalizes on the public's increasing interest in migratory birds and the national trend toward increasing the livability of urban areas, where more than 80 percent of Americans live. An Urban Treaty is a partnership agreement between a U.S. city and the Service for the purpose of conserving migratory birds through education and habitat improvement strategies. A one-to-one matching grant, up to $50,000, can be awarded to each participating city to fund education programs and habitat restoration and enhancement projects to

*To many people, birds represent their only day-to-day contact with the natural world. With environmentally aware citizens, urban communities play a crucial role in migratory bird conservation.*

Cedar Waxwing                                    USFWS/Dave Menke

Not only does the Service need to have reliable data on populations through harvest surveys, but also needs to learn more from management experiences. Last year the Service established the Adaptive Management and Assessment Team. This team coordinates with its partners and directs the application of adaptive resource management to migratory bird conservation. During FY 1999, the AMAT developed models and decision protocols for multiple duck stocks, investigated harvest strategies designed to produce population management feedback, and

conserve migratory birds. The first Urban Treaty and grant in the amount of $50,000 was awarded this year to the City of New Orleans, Louisiana. The Service anticipates partnering with five more cities over the next three years.

Throughout the Nation, the Service and affected States work cooperatively to address problems associated with an overabundance of a few migratory bird species. In cooperation with the States, the Service developed a Regional Snow Goose Management Action Plan for the

Central and Mississippi Flyways and initiated a public process to comprehensively address management alternatives to reduce the mid-continent populations of light geese (lesser snow geese and Ross' geese). The effect of management actions on mid-continent geese, as well as on non-target species, will be monitored and information will be used to develop other management alternatives, as necessary. Also, in the agricultural areas of the Pacific Northwest, the Service is investigating agricultural depredation complaints attributed to overabundance of Canada geese. The Service implemented control measures in Oregon and Washington which will be evaluated for

waterfowl populations are up more than 10 percent from 1998 populations and there is increased concern about bird strikes with commercial and private aircraft. Following a near-fatal collision of a commercial air cargo plane with a flock of snow geese near Kansas City in March 1999, the Service assisted the National Transportation Safety Board with its participation on an "accident" team which recommended actions to reduce the risk of birds striking aircraft. Further, the Service initiated discussions with the Federal Aviation Administration on developing formal cooperative processes to allow various Federal agencies to deal with bird strikes. This will continue to be a

Green Tree Frog

USFWS/F. Eugene Hester

effectiveness as future population management tools. Further, Double-crested cormorant populations have increased significantly over the last several decades because of improved habitat and environmental quality. Most particularly, the Great Lakes population increased an average of 22 percent per year between 1970 and 1997. Concerns over the suspected impacts on important sport and commercial fisheries caused the Service to form a national assessment team this year. This team will lead the Service's comprehensive look at what actions the Service and its State partners can take to manage overabundant populations of Double-crested cormorants in the future.

The Service and its Federal partners also look at increases in bird populations and their effect on aircraft traffic. The 1999

high priority issue for the Service in coming years.

The Service is working closely with a wide variety of partners and through many public forums to investigate and resolve high priority and complex species conservation issues. One of the more troubling issues is the decline of amphibian populations and the documented malformations occurring in natural environments. A Federal task force was formed to determine the cause and extent of amphibian declines and malformations. Our partners include other Department of the Interior agencies, the State Department, EPA, the Forest Service, and the Department of Defense. The Task Force on Amphibian Declines and Deformities suspects that one of the major causes of amphibian population declines is loss of suitable habitat. The Service is also a member of the new Partners in Amphibian and Reptile Conservation (PARC). PARC is modeled after the Partners in Flight program for Neotropical migratory birds. Membership includes government agencies, conservation groups, and industry. PARC's mission is "to conserve amphibians, reptiles, and their habitats as integral parts of our ecosystem and culture through proactive and coordinated public/private partnerships." At the regional and field level, the Service is also involved in amphibian conservation through conducting contaminant-related surveys on National Wildlife Refuges in the northeast, midwest, southwest, and Pacific coast regions. Workshops held in conjunction with the Department of Defense have also been organized to raise the sensitivity of military communities and silviculture industries to the plight of amphibian populations. Through these workshops, our partners are learning to monitor amphibians, to use new management methods to minimize impacts, and to conserve habitat.

Another complex problem is the fact that birds collide with communication towers. Not only are migratory birds lost but also damage to communication towers disrupts services to the public. The Service and members of industry and environmental groups want to minimize or avoid bird collisions. This summer the Service and 42 stakeholders met in Washington, D.C. at the environmental dispute resolution groups, RESOLVE, to begin discussions, to enhance understanding, and to form a working group to investigate and find solutions to bird collisions. The Service will continue to participate with a broad array of industry and environmental interest groups to continue to focus wildlife conservation issues, focus national information needs, and to design solutions to such complex conservation issues throughout the Nation.

Global wildlife conservation relies on international cooperation, education and enforcement at all levels. Not only is the Service advising foreign governments, but also the Service is a catalyst for community conservation action at the individual and local level in foreign Nations. For example, the African Elephant Conservation Fund, a small grants program administered by the Service, recently sponsored applied research and community conservation activities in Amboseli National Park, Kenya. Researchers collared elephants and conducted aerial surveys of the seasonal movements and distribution of

elephants in order to understand how to relieve elephant overcrowding in the national park. The data gathered also helped our work with local Masai communities to help reduce competition between elephants and humans for common resources.

This year, the inaugural year of the Asian Elephant Conservation Fund, activities are underway to gather data on human-elephant conflicts in Bukit Barisan Selatan National Park, Lampung Province, Sumatra, Indonesia. Much work remains to be done to help support declining Asian elephant populations and mediate human/elephant conflicts. Information gained from this project will help park managers decide how best in the future to manage crop loss caused by the elephants, how to implement survey and monitoring techniques for elephant management plans, and how to train forestry guards that will help prevent poaching.

Most Americans are aware that tigers are vanishing from the wild, and that the next hundred years may find the only world's remaining tigers in zoos. To help protect wild tigers and encourage their survival into the next millennium, the Rhinoceros and Tiger Conservation Fund is supporting a project for one of the most endangered of the five living tiger subspecies. The South China tiger makes its home in southern and central China, but is in immediate danger of becoming extinct in the wild due to deforestation and poaching. Populations have declined from an estimated 4,000 in 1949 to approximately 20-30 in 1998. The Rhinoceros and Tiger Conservation Fund is providing assistance to determine the present distribution of the South China tiger and its prey in the wild, information that otherwise would not be available but is critical to protecting this subspecies.

The Service has a long history of collaboration and information exchange with Russia to protect shared species and their habitat. This year biologists from Kamchatka and Sakhalin benefitted from Service assistance in an effort to conserve wild salmon populations. The information shared is particularly critical since it assists in the restoration of salmon populations in the Pacific Northwest. Also, the Service's support of the Russian nature reserve system almost doubled in 1999 as new funding helped support 16 nature reserves and 5 national parks in Russia. Small grants provided basic equipment necessary to combat poaching and maintain habitat for sturgeon, cranes, snow leopards and other species. Without

## Operation Chameleon - Uncovering An International Smuggling Ring

*Operation Chameleon*, a five-year probe uncovered illegal trafficking that targeted some of the world's most imperiled reptiles. This case documented a black market that spans six continents, with 22 people from the United States, Canada, Germany, the Netherlands, South Africa, Japan, Malaysia, and Hong Kong being indicted, arrested, or prosecuted. Assistance from the Justice Department's Environmental and Natural Resources Division, the U.S. Attorney's Office for the Middle District of Florida, and government authorities in Germany, the Netherlands, Belize, Mexico, and Canada, proved crucial throughout the Service's multi-year investigation.

One of the largest reptile importers in the U.S. conspired with German nationals to bring two species of highly protected snakes into the U.S. The Madagascar tree boa and ground boa both occur naturally only on Madagascar, an island off the southeastern coast of Africa, and are listed on Appendix I of the CITES. Listing of the boas on Appendix I indicates that they face extinction, and commercial traffic in such species is prohibited. In his January guilty plea, the Florida reptile dealer also admitted that he acquired smuggled exotic turtles from a Japanese national in 1996 and acknowledged illegal smuggling of more than 200 reptiles in total.

Swainson's Hawk

such assistance, Russian reserve managers could not have conducted even the minimal conservation activities required for these rare species.

Throughout the United States, the return of favorite birds from southern wintering grounds outside the U.S. is an eagerly awaited annual event. Yet hazards along the way often jeopardize their safe return. The Winged Ambassadors program helps safeguard species such as the osprey and Swainson's hawk. For example, during the winters of 1995 and 1996, 20,000 Swainson's hawks died in Argentina. Research linked a pesticide to these deaths. Through the conservation efforts of the Service and its international partners in subsequent years, we documented only 200 deaths this year.

Elsewhere in the Western Hemisphere, the Service is expanding its "Centers of Excellence for Migratory Birds and Ecosystem Management," which offer short courses that train existing and future wildlife science, management and enforcement personnel in Central America in the principles of migratory bird conservation. A new reserve manager training program in Central America emphasizes the importance of maintaining bird habitat in the region, and scholarships have been provided to Latin American

Madagascar Tree

graduate students studying resident and migratory birds. Local groups in Argentina also were linked to the North America-wide network of shorebird conservationists, opening an important channel of information about shorebird migration in South America. The Service uses the educational vehicle provided by Winged Ambassadors to strengthen conservation programs abroad and increase opportunities for them to become self-sustaining.

Reptiles and amphibians received a helping hand when the United States hosted the CITES Animals Committee Transport Working Group in Washington, D.C. Out of concern for the high injury and mortality rates of these animals shipped between countries, the goal of this meeting was to help improve humane transport for live reptiles and amphibians in international trade. Representatives included individuals from the Service, the animal welfare and conservation communities, the pet, airline and zoo industries, and the CITES Secretariat. The ground breaking meeting developed new standards for the humane transport of reptiles and amphibians which were proposed to the International Air Transport Association and put into effect globally this fiscal year. This is the first time CITES used a negotiated process to develop and implement a consensus resolution to a highly controversial international wildlife issue.

Last year the Service worked with partners to conserve goldenseal, a small forest understory plant highly valued for its medicinal properties. This year, in response to growing conservation concerns made evident by available biological and trade information, the Service met with State representatives on short notice prior to the 1999 harvest. The decision was made to limit ginseng exports to plants five years of age or older because the plant is mature at this age, and can produce viable seeds. Intervention on behalf of conserving the wild American ginseng was necessary to ensure that all exports of this important CITES Appendix II species are sustainable, without detriment to the survival of this species in the wild.

In addition, the Service worked with State conservation agencies and foreign governments and their wildlife departments to implement species management plans to ensure that commercial trade in protected species is both legal and biologically sustainable. State management programs conserve

CITES furbearers (lynx, bobcat, river otter), American alligator, and American ginseng.

Working with partners to build support for conserving species is proving to be an increasingly effective tool as the United States prepares this fiscal for the 11th Conference of the Parties to CITES (COP) to be held in Kenya in April 2000. The Service, with its partners, developed species proposals this year cooperatively through the CITES Coordination Committee — a multi-agency, interdisciplinary group made up of representatives of the Departments of Interior, Commerce, State, Justice, and Agriculture as well as the U.S. Agency for International Development, the U.S.

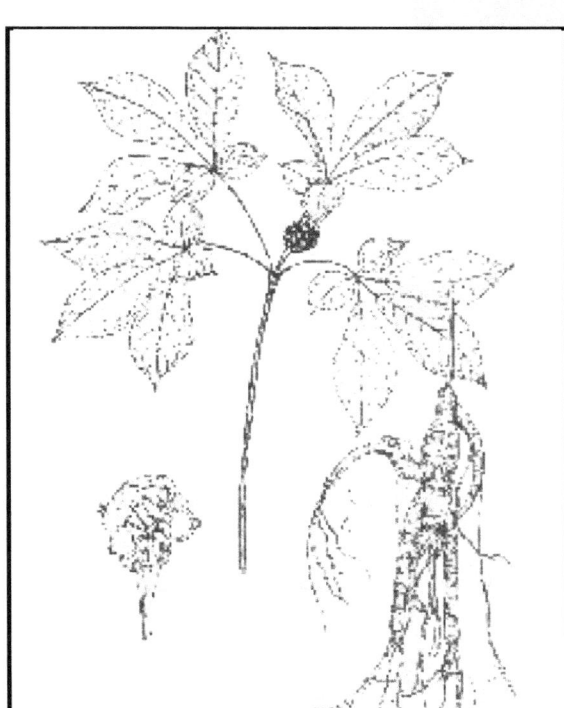

©University of Notre Dame

Trade Representative, and the Customs Service. State Fish and Game Agency representatives participated in the interagency process, thus enhancing Federal/State coordination on CITES preparations in FY 1999. A total of 54 countries were also consulted. Generally, the Service consults with counterparts abroad, but the process used this year was the first to include all possible stakeholders.

The Service's ability to conduct successful major international investigations involving the illegal trafficking of globally protected species is recognized worldwide. Special agents and wildlife inspectors

## FWS Establishes First-Ever Export Restrictions for Ginseng Roots

The Service took action to help ensure the long-term conservation and sustainable use of American wild ginseng. For the 1999 harvest, the Service issued export permits only for mature wild ginseng roots. These provisions did not affect the more than 2 million pounds of cultivated ginseng roots exported from the United States every year. In addition to helping ensure that wild ginseng plants have at least one season in which to reproduce, the new export condition is aimed at helping States within the species' range curb the poaching of wild roots by providing consistent law enforcement throughout the country.

Ginseng is an herbaceous perennial found in the understory of mixed hardwood forests of the northeastern, midwestern, and southeastern U.S. and in the Canadian provinces of Ontario and Quebec. It is long-lived, with a life expectancy of at least 60 years. Biologists are concerned that ginseng is not being allowed to reach maturity in the wild and that very few plants remain.

In 1975, because of its high demand for wild roots, American ginseng was listed on Appendix II of the Convention on International Trade in Endangered Species of Wild Fauna and Flora (CITES), a treaty that regulates trade in animals and plants to ensure the survival of wild populations.

## FWS works cooperatively with private landowners to...

monitor the legal international wildlife trade and interdict illegal importations and exportations of Federally protected fish, wildlife and plants. Wildlife traffickers increasingly use the international mail system and shift their trade routes to circumvent Service enforcement efforts. Controlling illegal trafficking of wildlife is facilitated by the use of task force operations that target specific shipments, industries, or methods of transport. Public outreach efforts at airports, ports and border crossings inform wildlife consumers of the long-term consequences of their wildlife purchases. The Service has developed partnerships with international conservation organizations, international inter-agency coalitions, and CITES countries, enhancing enforcement efforts to protect species of mutual concern.

### Conserving Habitat

Accomplishments in species conservation are intertwined with and, in many cases, dependent on the benefits associated with habitat conservation. Because fish and wildlife are mobile, habitat loss, degradation, and fragmentation are key factors affecting fish and wildlife populations. In this subsection, the Service highlights its work with its partners to protect, restore and manage priority habitats in sufficient quality and quantity for the benefit of fish, wildlife and

plant species and the healthy ecosystems upon which they depend for survival.

The most visible habitat protection system of the Service, the National Wildlife Refuge System (NWRS), provides a national network of lands and waters that serves as a secure home for fish and wildlife and plants. These refuges provide a lifeline for millions of migratory waterfowl; open spaces for elk, pronghorn, and caribou; and wild niches for the rare and endangered. The National Fish Hatchery System (NFHS) is also part of the Service's land system or habitat base. Together these key systems contribute to the overall success of ecosystem restoration.

This year, the Service began implementing many of the recommendations made in its 1998 Biological Needs Assessment (BNA), a document which recommended specific actions the NWRS could take to create and implement a comprehensive biological program integrating sound principles of wildlife management into all refuge operations, and ensuring Service compliance with the National Wildlife Refuge System Improvement Act of 1997. These actions bring the NWRS closer to more consistent biological staffing among regions, more consistent and standardized wildlife surveys, better training and more professionalism among refuge biologists, and better "quality control" for refuge biology through periodic site evaluations.

Snowgeese at Sunset

USFWS/E.Eugene Hester

Unique among Federal land management entities, the NWRS is the only land management system charged to conserve, restore, and manage habitats for the benefit of fish, wildlife, and plants. In FY 1999, the NWRS actively managed many of the habitats under its control, as shown in the following table:

| FY '99 NWRS Management Activities | |
| --- | --- |
| # acres* | Management Activity |
| 1,106,200 | Water level management |
| 105,600 | Moist soil management |
| 80,400 | Grassland managements |
| 174,900 | Farmed/cropped |
| 265,500 | Prescribed burned |

* Approximate

These and other management activities are aimed at keeping habitat in a vigorous and healthy state, increasing its attractiveness and utility to wildlife.

The Service increased prevention and control of invasive species that are threatening fish and wildlife and their habitats. An estimated six million acres of Service lands are infested with terrestrial weed species. The Service has joined with other Federal agencies under Executive Order 13112, signed on February 3, 1999 to battle against invasive species. In addition during FY 1999, the Service compiled a list of invasive species prevention and control projects on all units of the NWRS; coordinated with the Western Governor's Association to discuss issues, needs, and objectives in support of the Association's invasive species initiative; and developed and managed the new Service Invasive Species Web Page at http://INVASIVES.FWS.GOV.

Under mission goal 2, Conserving Habitat Through a Network of Lands and Waters, and strategic goal 2.1 entitled, "Habitat Conservation on Service Lands," the Service set a goal this year to meet the identified habitat needs of Service lands by ensuring that 93,567,296 acres (total acreage managed by FWS) are protected, of which 3,317,957 acres will be restored or enhanced.

The Service met its habitat needs goal by expanding the number of acres managed in the NWRS to 93,628,301 acres. Because of weather imacts, the Service met only 97 percent of its planned NWRS habitat improvement goal by restoring or

enhancing approximately 3.2 million acres in FY 1999.

Under this same strategic goal, the Service set a goal to complete 80 percent of contaminated cleanup projects on its lands according to their original schedule. Contaminant cleanup significantly contributes to the Service being able to provide quality habitat for fish and wildlife resources. This goal was met by completing all of the 24 scheduled cleanup projects for this year.

The Service will continue to have the NWRS and the NFHS serve as the examples for ecosystem stability in areas throughout the country and as critical tools to ecosystem recovery. But the Service recognizes that these systems cannot do the job alone. The primary reason for species to be listed under the ESA is the loss of habitat. According to a 1993 study by the Association for Biodiversity Information and The Nature Conservancy, half of listed threatened and endangered species have at least 80 percent of their habitat on private lands. The Service is committed to encouraging private landowners to manage their lands to help stabilize ecosystems, which in turn helps prevent species from declining to the point where protection under the ESA is necessary.

During FY 1999, the ESA Landowner Incentive Program provided $5 million to implement conservation actions. Twenty two projects from across the Nation were selected for funding, out of 145 proposals received. Conservation actions benefitted endangered birds in Hawaii, declining albatross species in Alaska, Northern Idaho ground squirrels, and lesser prairie chickens in New Mexico, Texas, and Oklahoma.

*...help them manage their lands to stabilize ecosystems.*

Chollas Cactus                                                    USFWS Photo

## Another Successful Year of Habitat Restoration

The Partners for Fish and Wildlife Program and the Coastal Program have continued their tradition of working in partnership with others to restore and protect fish and wildlife habitat in 1999. A quick tour of projects around the Nation shows how both programs share a commitment to conservation of habitats for trust species.

In the northeast, the Coastal Program worked with partners in Maryland to implement phase one of the Poplar Island restoration project. Poplar Island was a single 800-acre island in 1848 but, through erosion, had been split into four fragments now totaling 5 acres in size. This is the first large-scale project in the Chesapeake Bay to use dredged material for habitat restoration. When complete, the project will have restored more than 1,100 acres of wetland and upland habitat important for waterfowl, shorebirds and wading birds.

In New Jersey, the Partners Program is restoring 452 acres of estuarine marsh invaded by a species of common reed. Through the judicial use of herbicides, prescribed burning, and hydrological modifications, the project will allow native vegetation to become reestablished and improve habitat for anadromous fish, water birds, raptors, and furbearers.

Heading down to North Carolina, the Coastal Program and its partners are removing Rains Dam which will restore access to 49 miles of spawning and rearing habitat for six species of anadromous fish including shad and striped bass. This project complements two other successful dam removal projects (Quaker Neck Dam Removal and Cherry Hospital Dam Removal) that have restored access to 1,000 miles and 54 miles of fish spawning habitat respectively.

Moving on to the Great Lakes region, the Partners Program worked with a private landowner along the Kaskaskia River, in

Richard Harms Project - Lower end of restored oxbow          USFWS Photo

Illinois, to restore a 7-acre oxbow wetland by removing invading woody species and excess sediments, establishing nesting islands, and planting native vegetation. The restored habitat is now suitable for waterfowl and other migratory birds, fish, other aquatic species, and local wildlife.

Looking westward to Idaho, the Partners Program is restoring Twin Creek, a degraded creek that had once been habitat for the endangered bull trout. The Service is working with the landowners and other partners to remove the cattle from the creek, provide an alternate water source, reconstruct the stream's natural meanders, and plant native vegetation. Once restoration is complete this fall, the creek will be a suitable spawning ground for over 200 bull trout.

In Albuquerque, New Mexico, the Partners Program worked with many partners to restore an urban wetland along the Rio Grande. The land is part of an urban park visited by approximately 120,000 people a year. In the short time period since its completion, the project has been a breeding and feeding ground for waterfowl and shorebirds, and has also been used by other wildlife including birds of prey, kingfishers, deer and other mammals. As the wetland matures, it may be used by neotropical migratory birds such as the southwestern willow flycatcher.

The Texas Coastal Program has partnered with the State and National Marine Fisheries Service to protect and restore seagrass meadows in Texas' mid-coast region. Seagrasses provide critical nursery habitats for finfish and shellfish. Damage from boats has made thousands of acres of

Restoring Habitat                               USFWS/Will Roach

seagrass meadows vulnerable to erosion. By marking boat channels, providing boater information at marinas and boat ramps, planting sprigs, and injecting nutrients, approximately 10,000 acres of seagrasses will benefit. This is the first time that these highly successful techniques developed in Florida have been used in Texas.

Finally, heading to Alaska, the Partners program worked with landowners along Willow Creek, using innovative bioengineering techniques to stabilize the stream bank and restore native vegetation. The restored stream bank and resulting improved in-stream habitat will provide important habitat for moose as well as five species of Pacific salmon and three species of resident fish in this south central region.

Habitat Conservation Plans protect listed species while allowing necessary economic activity. HCPs are initiated by a developer, local government or other non-Federal entity as part of the application requirements for obtaining a permit under Section 10 of the ESA for the incidental take of a listed species. Applicants can explore different methods of achieving compliance with the ESA and choose the method that best suits them. With the added HCPs finalized in FY 1999, the total number of HCPs now number 250, covering approximately 11.6 million acres of land, 200 listed species, and many unlisted species.

Through the Cooperative Endangered Species Conservation Fund, the Service provides grants to State and local governments to integrate conservation planning and habitat protection into local land use planning and decision making. This year over $7.5 million was made available to the States for endangered species conservation. An additional $6 million was provided to acquire lands in support of HCPs. Projects funded under this program have resulted in significant habitat gains for fish and wildlife resources. For example, the State of Florida is monitoring recovery plans for populations of 13 listed plants that are found nowhere else in the world. The Oklahoma Department of Wildlife Conservation is conserving fragile Ozark cave ecosystems and recovering the endangered Ozark big-eared bat and gray bat through the construction of bat-friendly gates to prevent human disturbance during sensitive hibernation and breeding periods. On Block Island, Rhode Island, and Nantucket Island, Massachusetts, the State Wildlife agencies are restoring habitat for the endangered American burying beetle and reestablishing beetle populations on the islands from captive breeding facilities at several zoos in New England.

In FY 1999, the Service encouraged both private and public landowners to protect and restore habitat through both the Coastal Program and Partners for Fish and Wildlife Program. Both programs benefit migratory birds, threatened and endangered species, and provide improved habitat or access for anadromous and interjurisdictional fish, and other aquatic species. These programs effectively triple their capacity to restore and conserve habitat by leveraging funds from other partners.

Through the National Coastal Wetlands Conservation Grants Program, the Service provided over $9.7 million in grants to States and territories for acquisition, restoration, management and enhancement of coastal wetlands in 1999. Nineteen projects in 10 coastal States protected and/or restored 30,890 acres of coastal habitat. In Texas, for example, the Coastal Grants program provided funds to the Parks and Wildlife Department to restore 169 acres of intertidal marsh, submerged aquatic beds, salt flats, and high marsh on Galveston Island, a barrier island in Galveston Bay. Several Federally-listed species benefitted from this project, including the piping plover and Kemp's ridley and loggerhead sea turtles.

Working in concert with the U.S. Coral Reef Task Force in 1999, the Service continued its role as a leader in managing

Water Lillies                        USFWS/Ryan Hagerty

and protecting corals and their habitat. By enforcing trade restrictions, protecting against adverse effects from coastal development projects, and fostering conservation partnerships worldwide, the Service seeks to preserve coral reef ecosystems for future generations to cherish. Also, through collaborative habitat conservation efforts this year, the Navassa Island Refuge in Puerto Rico was added to the NWRS. The island and the submerged habitat around the refuge are biologically rich and will be protected and managed to preserve their remarkable character. The Service now manages 20 refuges that include or are adjacent to coral reefs, and has approximately 1.5 million acres of coral under its management authority.

## FWS now manages 20 refuges that include or are adjacent to coral reefs, and has approximately 1.5 million acres of coral under its management authority.

### Enforcing International Trade Restrictions to Protect Corals and Other Marine Species

An investigation of illegal trafficking in coral resulted in the criminal convictions of a Tarpoon Springs, Florida, man and his business for smuggling internationally protected corals from the Philippines to the United States. The guilty verdicts represent what Justice Department officials believe to be the first federal felony convictions for smuggling protected coral species. The defendant, and his business were indicted along with the owner and operator of a seashell and souvenir exporting business located in Cebu City, Republic of the Philippines. The U.S. is seeking the extradition of the Philippines supplier. The pair were smuggling protected corals and seashells into the U.S. by circumventing U.S. and Philippine laws as well as international trade restrictions that protect corals and other marine species.

In July 1997 a Service wildlife inspector intercepted a 40-foot shipping container packed with some 350 boxes and packages of coral and seashells in Tampa, Florida. Service special agents and U.S. Customs Service officers documented a series of transactions between the two conspirators that extended back to 1991. The Florida businessman could spend up to five years in jail and be fined up to $250,000 for each of three felony convictions; his company faces fines up to $500,000 per count.

Commercial exploitation is a serious threat to the continued viability of the world's coral reefs, nearly 60 percent of which are considered at risk because of human activities. Dangers range from illegal trade and destructive fishing practices to coastal development and marine pollution. Large-scale degradation of reefs has already occurred in east Africa, south and southeast Asia, parts of the Pacific, and the Carribean. Concern for reef conservation prompted the Phillippines to ban the export of corals in 1977. Many of the species targeted by the defendant and his alleged supplier (which include blue, organpipe, branch, brush, staghorn, finger, brown stem, mushroom and feather corals) have been listed on Appendix I the CITES since 1985. Such species may not be legally traded without export permits from the country of origin.

USFWS/Anja G. Burns

Our work depends on our ability to build strong relationships with our Federal partners. In FY 1999, the Service strengthened relations with the EPA through a truly unique partnership between the two agencies. EPA funds Service biologists to participate with their Environmental Response Team in the early planning stages of remediation at Superfund sites to ensure that fish and wildlife resource concerns are addressed. Service biologists are stationed in two of the EPA Regions and at the Environmental Response Team Center to ensure healthy habitat for endangered species, migratory birds, anadromous fish, marine mammals, and other wildlife resources.

In another example of Federal cooperation, the Service provided natural resource information to the Federal Energy Regulatory Commission which ordered the removal of the Edwards Dam, restoring important ecological riverine habitat in the Kennebec River in Maine. The Edwards Dam blocked 17 miles of the Kennebec River for over 160 years, which reduced instream flows and water quality, prevented fish migration, and killed fish that passed through dam power generators. With the removal of the 917-foot long dam, anadromous fish (Atlantic salmon, American shad, river herring, striped bass, Atlantic sturgeon, rainbow smelt and the endangered shortnose sturgeon) will be able to reach historic spawning grounds. This landmark decision, which was the first FERC ordered dam removal, can expand recreational and commercial fishing opportunities in this watershed.

Also, significant fish and wildlife habitat was preserved during an expansion project for U.S. Highway 12 in Wisconsin. The State's Department of Transportation, with information provided by the Service, minimized impacts to the 50,000-acre Baraboo Range National Natural Landmark. This landmark is a part of the 144,000-acre Baraboo Hills, the largest contiguous block of southern upland forest in the Midwest. Through the use of scenic easements, the cooperation between the State and the Service ensured protection of the unique resource values of the Baraboo Range and preservation of interior forest habitats that are critical to interior forest-nesting birds.

Through collaboration among 15 Federal agencies and bureaus, of which the Service was one, an award winning book was developed to help landscape architects fully consider fish and wildlife resources

during project planning and construction. The award-winning book entitled, "Stream Corridor Restoration: Principles, Processes and Practices," was published in FY 1998 and received the American Society of Landscape Architects' prestigious "President's Award of Excellence in Communication" for 1999.

Landscape approaches to conservation, whether at the individual or local site level or across continents, are essential to conserve wetlands. Since the inception of the North American Waterfowl Management Plan in 1986, the Service has worked with regional, national and international partners to protect and restore habitat throughout the continent for waterfowl and other wildlife that use wetlands. In FY 1999, the second update to the 1986 Plan known as "Expanding the Vision" was completed and signed by

USFWS Photo

government representatives of Canada, Mexico, and the U.S. This update improves the ability of signatory countries to conserve waterfowl and their habitats by challenging participants to strengthen the use of their biological foundation, employ the application of a landscape approach, and forge broader alliances with other conservation initiatives, particularly those involving migratory birds. Further, the update established the North American Bird Conservation Initiative (NABCI). The NABCI builds on the existing structure of the Plan, which has conserved almost 5 million acres of habitat in the United States since 1986. The

*Landscape approaches to conservation are essential to conserve wetlands.*

NABCI was formed to broaden the Plan's bird conservation partnerships, enlarge the resources available for bird conservation, and increase the effectiveness of existing resources and partnerships.

In FY 1999, projects funded under the North American Wetlands Conservation Act's (NAWCA) standard grants program protected or restored 374,000 acres in the United States with the aid of more than $28.4 million in grant funds and over $189.9

is linked to the well-being of fish and wildlife populations and their habitats. This environmental information must be made accessible to the public in order to foster their responsible stewardship of these valuable resources. Also, private citizens, whose voluntary participation in fish and wildlife conservation, have laid a foundation on which the Service operates today and have contributed to the continuing conservation of fish and wildlife resources throughout the world.

Visitation to the NWRS is the most direct opportunity for the public to enjoy wildlife that the Service provides. In FY 1999, over 34 million people visited units within the National Wildlife Refuge System and over 1.9 million people visited facilities within the National Fish Hatchery System. Priority public uses are wildlife observation, hunting and fishing, interpretation, environmental education, and nature photography. Additional information on refuge visitation is in the Stewardship section of this report.

USFWS Photos

The Service enters into partnerships agreements with a wide variety of the public, as individuals and as organizations, at the national, regional, and local levels to benefit the NWRS and the Nation's wildlife resources. Partnerships bring additional skills and expertise into refuge operations. An important contribution to community partnerships was made by Congress this fiscal year with the passage of the National Wildlife Refuge System Volunteer and Community Partnership Enhancement Act of 1998 (P.L. 105-242) on October 5, 1998. The Act brings recognition and additional authorities to the Service's volunteer program, including authority to establish a Senior Volunteer Program, and added support for community partnerships and education programs.

*The Nation's ability to sustain ecosystems, and the natural heritage of fish and wildlife within them, increasingly ...*

million in partner funds. Through this partnership program, more than 1.2 million acres were protected and enhanced in Canada. Mexican projects typically include education and management plans affecting large biosphere reserves. The NAWCA small grants program affected more than 5,000 acres. Twenty-one projects were funded with $732,000 of grant funds and $4.1 million of partner funds, representing a 5.6 to 1 partner-to-grant ratio.

### Linking Wildlife and People

The Nation's ability to sustain ecosystems, and the natural heritage of fish and wildlife resources within them, will increasingly depend on the public's active participation in the stewardship of these valuable resources. A growing number of the public lack first-hand experience with fish and wildlife resources in their natural setting. Thus, the Service provides environmental education to help the public understand how their well-being

The resources and expertise made available to the Service through partnerships is wide ranging. Notable partners include the National Fish and Wildlife Foundation, the National Wildlife Refuge Association, the National Audubon Society, the Cooperative Alliance for Refuge Enhancement (CARE), Safari Club International, Ducks Unlimited, Inc., the Outdoor Writers Association, the Student Conservation Association, the American Association of Retired Persons (AARP), numerous grassroots partners commonly known as Refuge Support (Friends) Groups, and many others.

CARE consists of a coalition of 17 sportsmen's and environmental groups seeking to raise awareness of the impacts of insufficient operating funds and the ensuing threat to wildlife conservation and visitor services on national wildlife refuges. This unique support group includes organizations as diverse as The Wilderness Society and the National Rifle Association, and has become an influential voice for the NWRS.

New community-based "Refuge Support Groups" are being developed on a continuing basis nationwide. Groups consist of local citizens who have established community partnerships that supports the mission of their hometown national wildlife refuge. Because group memberships are derived from private citizens in communities across the Nation, the NWRS is supported by a growing constituency which reflects a rich diversity of wildlife conservation interests. This wealth of ideas, skills, talents, and expertise being woven into friends groups will both strengthen and enrich the NWRS.

To help with establishing Friends groups, a small but enthusiastic group of individuals from 40 community partnerships met and formed their own coalition to "jump start" the campaign for developing Friends groups. Their accomplishments are many and include developing a training course for recruiting and organizing local citizens, publishing a directory of existing partnerships, and creating an instructional booklet for those groups interested in beginning 501(c)(3) nonprofit organizations. This special group also established "mentoring teams" which traveled to communities near units of the NWRS (9 visits in FY 1999), providing customized guidance to local citizens to start Friends organizations. Congress continued to support the Friends Initiative in the form of a $125,000 budget allocation to provide small grants from $500 to $5,000 to assist local Friends groups. Serving as a Friends Initiative partner, the National Fish and Wildlife Foundation administers the grants. Over 90 proposals from 28 States were received from Friends groups trying to better connect the refuge to the community.

The National Audubon Society continues its support through local support groups, called Audubon Refuge Keepers (ARK), which are involved in all aspects of refuge enhancement, from habitat restoration to environmental education. More than 75 ARK groups have been established to assist local refuges. The ARK program is an integral part of Audubon's Wildlife Refuge Campaign which works to build a

broader nationwide understanding and appreciation for the NWRS.

Cooperating Associations are nonprofit partner corporations which receive authorization through the National Wildlife Refuge System Administration Act of 1966 and the Refuge Recreation Act of 1962, as amended. There are currently 38 Cooperating Associations operated on 60 field stations. Cooperating Associations work with the Service to create, produce and sell educational publications, maps, visual aids, and natural resource related articles, and services. These interpretive and educational materials and services enhance visitor understanding of the natural, cultural, and recreational resources of the area as well as the mission of the Service. Sales from bookstores, managed and operated by Cooperating Associations, help fund many of the Service's interpretive, educational, recreational and biological initiatives.

Volunteer assistance in FY 1999 equated to hundreds of full time employees with volunteers performing services valued at over $20 million for the NWRS. More than 50 percent of volunteer time supported public education and recreation.

Under mission goal three, linking wildlife and people through fostering public use

*...depends on the active participation of the public in the stewardship of these valuable resources.*

Volunteers Help Manage NWRS Resources                          USFWS Photo

and enjoyment of fish and wildlife resources, and strategic goal 3.2 entitled, "Opportunities for Participating in Conservation on Service Lands," the Service set a goal to increase volunteer participation hours in Service programs by 26 percent and for refuges and hatcheries to have 43 new Friends groups above those existing in 1997. The Service met 90 percent of the volunteer participation goal in FY 1999. The lower hours may be an indication that refuges are reaching the limits of current staff abilities to assist volunteers and to oversee volunteer contributions. Further, the Service predicted that 107 Friends groups would be in place in FY 1999 to help meet this and other goals. The Service exceeded this goal with the support of 120 Friends

Chincoteague Volunteer                    USFWS Photo

groups in place in FY 1999. The use of the term "Friends" groups refers to all refuge and hatchery support groups, which have many names, such as cooperative associations, Audubon refuge keepers, friends, and natural history associations.

In delivering this goal, the Service is integrating volunteer activities into its resource management actions. Volunteers conduct fish and wildlife surveys, present interpretive programs to visitors, help stock fish from hatcheries, maintain equipment and facilities, and staff information desks at visitor centers. The Service hosts workshops and training sessions for volunteers and prospective partners to increase the effectiveness of volunteer partnerships, to strengthen ties with local communities, and to assist in improving the work of existing and new Friends organizations.

The National Fish Hatchery System (NFHS) also provides outreach programs to help promote public environmental awareness and involve the public in aquatic resource stewardship and fishery management. As a result, over three million people visit Service fish hatcheries annually. Many visitors are attracted by the opportunities that National Fish Hatcheries provide in aquatic education. Each year thousands of students from private and public schools take advantage of outdoor laboratories and learning centers at Service hatcheries. The ages of the students span almost 20 years, beginning with pre-school children from daycare centers and ending with graduate students from major colleges and universities.

Many of the outreach and education programs for the NFHS are conducted by volunteers who recognize the important role hatcheries play in forming proper environmental values and ethics in Americans of all ages. More than 3000 volunteers contribute over 61,000 hours of their time annually to assist with outreach and education activities in the NFHS.

Fish hatcheries also provide wonderful opportunities for adults and children to commune with nature. Hundreds of thousands of visitors, especially parents and grandparents who want their youngsters to better appreciate fish and fishing, come simply to see fish firsthand. To encourage these experiences, many Service hatcheries have aquaria, special windows and stations where visitors can see several kinds of fishes, and various displays that explain the importance of being good stewards of our Nation's aquatic resources. Also, our hatcheries host special events, like fishing derbies and special social gatherings, where visitors are provided other opportunities to learn about aquatic resources and participate in programs designed to strengthen public awareness of the importance of caring for fishery resources. National Fishing Week, an annual activity designed for outreach purposes, is actively supported by the Fisheries Program. Fishing clinics, display aquariums, demonstrations, and environmental education sessions are highlights of this event. These events not only expose children and adults to the joys of recreational fishing, but also illustrate the importance of a quality environment necessary to provide these opportunities.

Service Fishery facilities are linked to many colleges and universities through

## Law Enforcement is Essential to Every Aspect of Fish and Wildlife Conservation

The Service is responsible for enforcing U.S. and international laws and treaties that protect wildlife resources. Service law enforcement today focuses on potentially devastating threats to wildlife resources — illegal trade, unlawful commercial exploitation, habitat destruction, and environmental contaminants. Program efforts help Americans understand and obey wildlife protections laws and assist international, State, and Tribal counterparts to conserve wildlife resources. This work includes:

* Infiltrating international smuggling rings that target imperiled animals
* Preventing the unlawful commercial exploitation of protected U.S. species
* Safeguarding critical habitat for endangered species and preventing habitat loss
* Preserving legitimate hunting opportunities in partnership with States
* Inspecting wildlife shipments to intercept illegal trade
* Fulfilling global conservation responsibilities with international counterparts
* Training other federal, state, and foreign law enforcement officers
* Analyzing evidence and solving wildlife crimes with the tools of forensic science
* Distributing information to increase public understanding of wildlife conservation

When fully staffed, the Service employs a corps of 252 special agents and 93 wildlife inspectors. Service special agents are plainclothes criminal investigators with full Federal law enforcement authority; they work in settings that range from major cities to one-person duty stations that cover some of the few remaining wilderness areas left in the country. Common targets range from international smuggling rings to illegal guiding operations.

The methods and roles of Service special agents are varied and effective. They are key players on Service ecosystem teams and use their expertise to support species reintroduction programs. They pursue habitat destruction cases and help promote and enforce Habitat Conservation Plans under the ESA. Special agents conduct training on wildlife law enforcement for State and Tribal officers as well as for enforcement officers overseas. They conduct patrol and surveillance operations to enforce federal migratory game bird hunting regulations, support drug eradication and interception efforts on lands managed by the Service, and provide investigative expertise when wildlife crimes occur on national wildlife refuges. Special agents forge partnerships with industry groups to remove hazards to migratory birds and other wildlife caused by oil pits, powerlines, pesticides, and mining operations, and investigate those who ignore their obligations to wildlife.

USFWS/Ryan Hagerty

The tools of the Service's law enforcement program include the Clark R. Bavin National Fish and Wildlife Forensics Laboratory, which conducts scientific analyses to support Federal, State, and international investigations of wildlife crime. The Service further maintains a National Wildlife Property Repository, which supplies abandoned and forfeited wildlife items to schools, universities, and museums for public education, and the National Eagle Repository, which meets the needs of Native Americans for eagles and eagle feathers for religious use.

*Visitors are provided opportunities to learn about aquatic resources . . .*

USFWS/F. Eugene Hester

*. . . and to strengthen their appreciation of these resources.*

formal cooperative programs under which undergraduate and graduate students conduct research or work part-time at hatcheries. Under an education program begun in 1994, many of our National Fish Hatcheries initiated cooperative programs with secondary schools with the goal to provide instruction in fish biology, aquaculture, fishing, and ecosystem stewardship. Curricula developed include laboratory analysis of fish specimens, principles of applied fisheries management, and opportunities for students to learn hatchery production techniques.

The proper maintenance of facilities within the NWRS and the NFHS is a major concern of the Service, considering facility condition and its role in providing the public access to the valuable fish, wildlife and plant resources protected within these systems. Refuge water management facilities, fish hatcheries, visitor centers, buildings, roads, dikes, dams, bridges, and other facilities represent a major investment by the American people in resources that support the mission of the Service.

The deferred maintenance estimate for facilities in the NWRS is approximately $675 million, plus or minus 15 percent, placing the estimate within a range of approximately $575 million to $775 million. The deferred maintenance estimate for facilities within the NFHS is approximately $255 million, plus or minus 15 percent, placing the estimate within a range of approximately $217 million to $293 million. Based on condition assessment surveys of maintenance needs of Service facilities, the estimates that deferred maintenance for aggregate facilities within both systems is estimated at approximately $930 million, plus or minus 15 percent, placing the range between approximately $790 million and $1.1 billion for all facilities under the jurisdiction of the Service. The Service recognizes that estimating deferred

maintenance requires the professional judgement of numerous site managers gathering information from multiple sources. These estimates can represent average costs among several sources or can be the costs of the last estimate increased over time to accommodate inflation since the last estimate. Each method is acceptable; however, estimates may vary by 15 percent above or below any discrete number provided.

The Service's estimates of deferred maintenance are aggregate estimates for all facilities and for all property related to facility operations. The aggregate estimates do not include construction of facilities not previously existing, or significant expansion of existing facilities, or major upgrades of structures, but rather are estimates of bringing existing facilities into a functional or acceptable operating condition. Maintenance of a minor, custodial nature, including grass mowing, snow removal, grounds maintenance, routine equipment servicing (excluding preventive maintenance), and janitorial services are not included in the Service's estimate. Equipment replacement is also excluded from this estimate.

USFWS/F. Eugene Hester

A standard measure of condition for facilities is a ratio of the estimates of deferred maintenance needs to the replacement value of such facilities, known as the Facilities Condition Index (FCI), which is a commonly used industry measure of condition. Estimates of deferred maintenance needs represent those field station maintenance needs that have not been funded for at least one year. The replacement value is the estimate for replacing these facilities at today's costs. The FCI illustrates the percentage of its capital amount that an institution would have to spend to eliminate the deferred maintenance. If the ratio of accumulated deferred maintenance estimate to replacement value is from 0 percent to 5 percent, the condition of the facilities is considered as "good." If the ratio is greater than 5 percent but less than 10 percent, the condition is considered as "fair" and if the ratio is 10 percent or greater, then condition is considered "poor." The replacement value for facilities within the NWRS is estimated at $4.5 billion and for the NFHS at $800 million, with a combined total of $5.3 billion. Based on condition assessment surveys conducted by the Service, the FCI for facilities within the NWRS is estimated at approximately 16.5 percent and for the NFHS at approximately 32 percent, with a combined FCI for all Service facilities estimated at approximately 19 percent. Therefore, the overall condition of Service facilities is "poor."

The FCI calculations in the preceding paragraph are based on the best information available to date. During FY 1999, the Service began an effort to improve data concerning the extent of real property owned and its replacement value. As a result, a more refined calculation of the FCI will be available next year.

Finally, the Service actively links wildlife and people through an aggressive outreach program. By arranging and providing media support for such major milestones as the proposed delisting of the American bald eagle and the Aleutian Canada goose, and the final delisting of the peregrine falcon this year, the Service helps the public understand the Nation's progress on conservation issues. In addition to assisting the news media accurately cover the conservation programs and accomplishments, the Service initiated a number of innovative ideas to reach new and different audiences with its conservation message. In cooperation with a major theater chain, the Service arranged for urban moviegoers to receive projected "preview" messages highlighting the wildlife-dependent recreational opportunities provided by the NWRS. Also, the Service's presence on the World Wide Web provides the public and all stakeholders with the most recent overview of the Service, its programs, and its work. Further, the Service provided every employee with a pocket guide to the Service, its programs, and its long-term goals and objectives. This pocket guide ensures better communications within the Service and provides employees with a useful information tool to better respond to information requests from the public we serve.

National Conservation Training Center
USFWS Photo

The Service has a proud tradition of working with its partners throughout the Nation and the world to effect solutions that benefit fish and wildlife resources and the habitat upon which they depend for survival. During FY 1999, as with every other year before, the Service has enjoyed the increasing support of the Congress, the President, and the American public so that we can all work to benefit our natural heritage and the world's fish and wildlife resources. We look forward to continuing to build new and nurture existing cooperative programs so that fish and wildlife management remains a useful and productive tool in conserving our valued fish and wildlife resources for future generations.

*FWS has a proud tradition of working with its partners to find solutions to environmental issues that benefit fish and wildlife resources and the habitats upon which they depend for survival.*

Cooperative Habitat Management
USFWS Photo

USFWS/L. David Mech

# Stewardship

*Stewardship Assets*

By law and treaty, the Service has national and international management and law enforcement responsibilities for migratory birds, threatened and endangered species, fisheries and many marine mammals. Also, the Service assists State and Tribal governments and other Federal agencies in protecting America's fish and wildlife resources. Further, the Service manages over 93 million acres in the National Wildlife Refuge System (NWRS) and the National Fish Hatchery System (NFHS). These lands and the fish and wildlife resources they support are valued for their environmental and cultural resources, for their educational and scientific benefits, for their recreational and scenic values, and for the revenue they provide to the Federal Government, States, and Counties.

## STEWARDSHIP LANDS

*Stewardship Lands and Facilities and Their Locations*

The Service manages land in all 50 States, some of the Pacific Islands, the Virgin Islands, Guam, and Puerto Rico. Over 80 percent of the acreage of the Service's land holdings are in Alaska. Lands within the NWRS include 521 refuge units, 200 Waterfowl Production Areas, and 50 Coordination Areas. Lands and facilities within the NFHS are comprised of 67 hatcheries, located within 34 States, and 16 other fish facilities such as Fish Health Centers and Fish Technology Centers. *Figure 1 displays the acres owned by the Service for all its land uses.* These lands are acquired through a variety of methods such as withdrawal from the public domain, fee title purchase, transfer of jurisdiction, donation, gift, exchange, and partial interest through agreements, easements, and leases. *Figure 2 shows the percentage of stewardship lands acquired through these different methods.* Lands are purchased through two primary sources of funding, the Migratory Bird Conservation Fund and the Land and Water Conservation Fund.

*Uses of Stewardship Lands*

Lands managed within the NWRS are used to conserve and manage fish, wildlife and plant resources for the benefit of present and future generations. The habitat protected is as diverse as the wild things living there. Service stewardship lands protect tundra, grasslands, deserts, forests, rivers, marshes, swamps, and remote islands - virtually every type of habitat and landscape found in the United States. The fish, wildlife and plants that live on refuges are the heritage of a wild America that was, and is. The Service watches over 700 species of birds, 220 species of mammals, 250 reptile and amphibian species, more than 1,000 species of fish, and countless species of invertebrates and plants. They come as flocks, herds, coveys, gaggles, schools, pairs and loners. Nearly 260 threatened and endangered species are found on Service lands, and it is on refuges and on hatcheries that they often begin their recovery and hold their own against extinction. The Service protects, restores, and manages this fish, wildlife, plant, land, and water heritage. We count it, study it, band it, mark it, and reintroduce it and we let wildlife come naturally by managing its home and its habitat. On many refuges the Service must restore what was ditched, drained and cleared and actively manage wetlands, grasslands, forests, and to a lesser extent, croplands to provide the variety of habitat needed by diverse fish and wildlife species. Control of invasive and exotic pest plants and animals is essential in order to retain or restore native fish, wildlife, and plants. Over three million acres of NWRS lands are restored and enhanced each year. While the needs of fish and wildlife must come first, refuges welcome those who want to enjoy the natural world, to observe or photograph wildlife, to hunt or to fish, or to study and learn about wildlife and their needs.

The National Wildlife Refuge System Improvement Act of 1997 emphasized wildlife recreation opportunities for

**ANNUAL STEWARDSHIP INFORMATION**
**FOR THE YEARS ENDED SEPTEMBER 30, 1999 AND 1998**
**(ACRES IN THOUSANDS)**

| | 1999 | | 1998 | |
|---|---|---|---|---|
| | SITES | ACRES | SITES | ACRES |
| National Wildlife Refuge System: | | | | |
| National Wildlife Refuges | 521 | 87,627 | 516 | 87,495 |
| Coordination Areas | 50 | 197 | 50 | 197 |
| Waterfowl Production Areas | 200 | 715 | 199 | 704 |
| Total, National Wildlife Refuge System | 771 | 88,539 | 765 | 88,396 |
| Other Land Uses: | | | | |
| National Fish Hatcheries (67) and Other Fish Facilities (16) | 83 | 16 | 83 | 14 |
| Total | 854 | 88,555 | 848 | 88,410 |

Figure 1

# Service Acquisitions

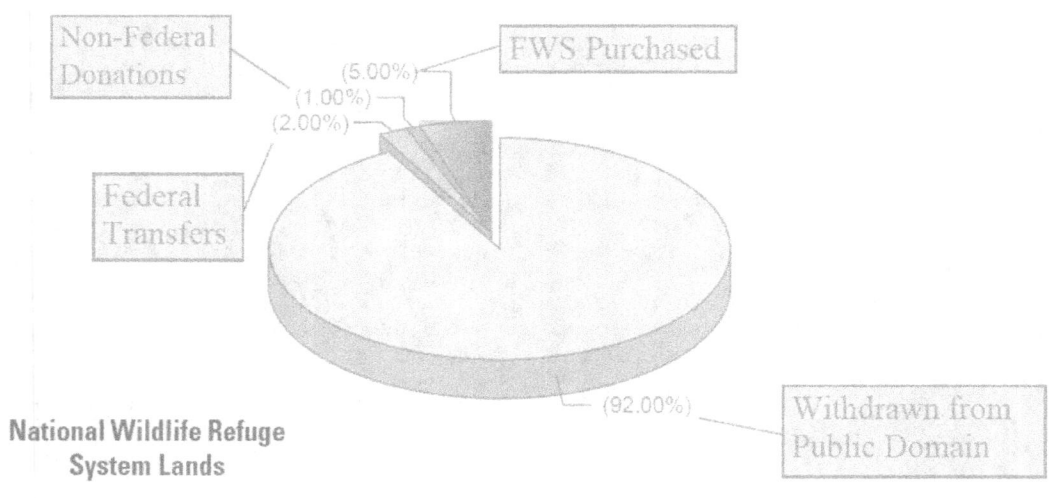

Non-Federal Donations (1.00%)

Federal Transfers (2.00%)

FWS Purchased (5.00%)

Withdrawn from Public Domain (92.00%)

**National Wildlife Refuge System Lands**

Figure 2

Americans in hunting, fishing, photography, wildlife observation, interpretation, and environmental education. The visitor programs at 37 refuges were significantly improved and expanded utilizing FY 1999 budget increases, including Don Edwards San Francisco Bay NWR, California; Kealia Pond NWR, Hawaii; Salt Plains NWR, Oklahoma; Brazoria NWR, Texas; Shiawasee NWR, Michigan; Neal Smith NWR, Iowa; Parker River NWR, Massachusetts; Petit Manan NWR, Maine; and Kodiak, Tetlin, and Kenai NWRs, Alaska. These projects included upgraded refuge orientation signs, improved hunting and fishing access, development of nature and canoe trails, and increased community outreach.

In FY 1999, two major draft policies affecting the NWRS were published in the Federal Register to seek public review and comment. These were the draft planning policy for the NWRS on August 13, 1999 and the draft compatibility policy on September 9, 1999. The draft planning policy stipulates that all NWRS units will be managed in accordance with approved Comprehensive Conservation Plans, developed with active public involvement. Each NWRS unit will develop a CCP by October 2012, which will be revised every 15 years thereafter, or sooner if necessary. CCPs will establish management strategies for achieving the purposes of the individual unit and its contribution to the mission of the NWRS. Since 1997, 9 CCPs have been completed, with 72 more plans underway nationwide, encompassing 122 stations.

The draft compatibility chapter establishes the process for determining whether existing and proposed uses of a unit of the NWRS are a compatible use. The draft policy ensures that compatibility, as a conservation standard, will be consistently applied and more understandable to the public. The policy defines a compatible use as a "wildlife-dependent recreational or any other use of a national wildlife refuge that, in the sound professional judgment of the Refuge Manager, will not materially interfere with or detract from the fulfillment of the National Wildlife Refuge System Mission or the major purposes of the affected national wildlife refuge." Prior to issuing a final compatibility determination, public review and comments will be considered by the Refuge Manager.

Another milestone in FY 1999 was publication of the "Fulfilling the Promise"

report, which reflects on where the NWRS has been, reviews the present, and presents a vision for the future. It was developed through the first-ever System Conference held in Keystone, Colorado in October 1998, attended by every Refuge Manager in the country, other Service employees, and scores of conservation organizations. "Fulfilling the Promise" provides 42 recommendations for the future direction of the System, and how it will meet its obligations to wildlife, habitat, and the public, as well as assuring that outstanding leadership is in place to guide

## *America's National Wildlife Refuges ...*

Clockwise from top left: USFWS/William Hartgrove; USFWS/Mark Ranzon; USFWS/David Vogel; USFWS/Tom Smylie

## *where wildlife comes naturally!*

the System in the coming years. The following excerpts exemplify what "Fulfilling the Promise" is all about:

Vision for the Future: Wildlife and Habitat - "The vision stresses the basic principles that wildlife comes first, that ecosystems, biodiversity and wilderness are vital concepts in refuge management, that refuges must be healthy, and that growth of the System must be strategic. The vision also recognizes a commitment to leadership and excellence in wildlife management, and a responsibility to share this leadership by being models for others to learn from and follow."

Vision for the Future: People - "The National Wildlife Refuge System of the next century will provide the American people a Legacy of Wildlife, a Place Where Visitors are Welcome, Opportunities for Stewardship, and a System to Appreciate."

## THE BLUE GOOSE

## ITS IMPORTANCE OFFICIALLY RECOGNIZED

The "Blue Goose" sign, being installed at Chincoteaque NWR in Virginia, has been used for generations to designate refuge boundaries. Former FWS employee Rachel Carson summarized the purpose of the Blue Goose sign with these words:

"Wild creatures, like men, must have a place to live. As civilization creates cities, builds highways, and drains marshes, it takes away, little by little, the land that is suitable for wildlife. As their space for living dwindles, the wildlife populations themselves decline. Refuges resist this trend by saving some areas from encroachment, and by preserving in them, or restoring where necessary, the conditions that wild things need in order to live."

Vision for the Future: Leadership - "The leadership vision for the System is to identify and develop America's Best and Brightest to staff the System, to maintain and build Esprit de Corps, and to strengthen the System Integrity of refuges and waterfowl production areas."

During FY 1999, the "Fulfilling the Promise" Implementation Team was established. Out of 128 action items identified in the Team's draft Implementation Plan, 10 were completed during FY 1999, with 49 more planned to be completed during FY 2000. The blue goose symbol, long associated with the NWRS, was officially recognized as a permanent design element for the NWRS, and was incorporated into Service Graphic Standards and the Sign Manual.

Stewardship of the Nation's fishery and aquatic resources, through the NFHS, has been a core responsibility of the Service for over 120 years. Although the Service does not own all the lands and facilities in the NFHS, the Service participates in managing units within the NFHS, which is comprised of National Fish Hatcheries,

USFWS Photo

Fish Health Centers, and Fish Technology Centers. Many of our hatcheries serve as outdoor laboratories for school groups, environmental organizations, and universities. Visitor Centers on many hatcheries provide public education

opportunities for the approximately three million visitors each year. Fish Health Centers focus on cooperative work conducted by Federal, State and Tribal fishery managers to identify and control fish pathogens and diseases, particularly in wild stocks. Fish Technology Centers emphasize scientific management of fish stocks and aquatic communities by improving technologies in fish propagation, broodstock management, stock assessment, and aquaculture. NFHS lands also provide refugia, technology development and captive propagation for over 30 species of threatened and endangered plants and animals, from Texas wild rice to Wyoming toads to Ozark cavefish. In addition to conservation, restoration, and management of fish and wildlife resources and their habitats, the NFHS provides recreational opportunities to the public, such as fishing, hiking, and birdwatching.

All programs contributing to stewardship actions on Service lands are tied to supporting the Service's mission — 'working with others to conserve, protect and enhance fish, wildlife, and plants and their habitats for the continuing benefit of the American people.' The Service also recognizes the role that our Federal, State, Tribal, and private partners play in building on the successes realized by the Service in conserving stewardship resources.

*Revenue from Stewardship Assets*

The Recreational Fee Demonstration Program is a highly successful endeavor for participating units of the NWRS. There were 10 new sites approved in FY 1999. Receipts for FY 1999 were in excess of $2,900,000 with an estimated 80 percent returned to the refuges where the funds were collected. To enhance the visitor experience, these funds are used to improve visitor services through restoring and maintaining trails, adding interpretive programs, improving signs, building accessible wildlife observation platforms, and upgrading of aquarium equipment.

Also, the Service makes payments to counties in which Service lands and holdings are located. Funding for these payments is derived from a combination of annual appropriations and revenues generated through the sale of products from Service lands incidental to habitat management, such as timber and oil and gas receipts. Payments to counties in FY 1999 totaled $16,606,174 which is 62 percent of full entitlement.

Further, the Service awards grants to States and Territories for fish and wildlife conservation purposes. In FY 1999, the Service awarded $191.2 million for the purposes of acquiring and improving lands and nonfederal physical properties, $129.1 million for purposes of hunter safety and other fish and wildlife use safety training and outreach, and $37.7 million for conducting biological investigations that will contribute to site-specific natural resource management decisions.

The Service's Federal Aid in Sport Fish Restoration and the Federal in Wildlife Restoration Programs are the mainstays of State fish and wildlife resource management efforts. Excise taxes, collected from manufacturers of equipment used in hunting and fishing, sport shooting on ranges, and on motorboat fuels, are deposited into trust funds for investment and then, after appropriate deductions, are apportioned to each State. In FY 1999 apportionments of Sport Fish and Wildlife Restoration funding for the States totaled $377,782,612. The last 5-year average apportionment to the States is over $179 million for wildlife and more than $230 million for sport fish restoration. Also in FY 1999, $5 million was made available for the new National Outreach and Communication Program authorized by the Transportation Equity Act for the 21st Century enacted last year. This law provides the 35 million anglers and 71 million boaters of America with additional resources over the next seven years for sport fisheries management and restoration. This is not a gift from Congress, but rather is the model "user-pays, user-benefits" program. Users contribute through revenues collected from motorboat and small engine fuels taxes and excise taxes on fishing tackle, electric trolling motors, flasher-type sonar fish finders, and import duties on fishing tackle and pleasure boats.

*Net Change in Stewardship Land Acreage from 1998 to 1999*

The Service has gained approximately 145,000 acres in stewardship lands that it owns. These FY 1999 acquisitions provide permanent protection for valuable wetland, riparian, coastal and upland habitat for fish, wildlife and plant species, including threatened and endangered species.

The Service added six new units to the National Wildlife Refuge System in FY 1999: Aroostook National Wildlife Refuge, Maine; Colorado River Wildlife Management Area, Utah; Lost Trail

National Wildlife Refuge, Montana; Navassa Island National Wildlife Refuge, Navassa Island; Shawangunk Grasslands National Wildlife Refuge, New York; and Whittlesey Creek National Wildlife Refuge, Wisconsin.

USFWS Photo

Aroostook National Wildlife Refuge is the former Loring Air Force Base, which the Defense Base Closure and Realignment Commission recommended for closure. Through the Base Closure process and our authority to request no-cost transfers from other Federal agencies, the Service received upland forested areas, wetland areas, brooks, beaver ponds, and associated riparian habitat and forested bog systems. This varied habitat supports many species of mammals, amphibians, reptiles, and fish. Although this unit entered the system late in FY 1998, the Service reports on this new addition for the first time this year.

The Colorado River Wildlife Management Area has an approved boundary that includes 10,000 acres on the combined river reaches of the Upper Colorado, Gunnison, and Green River systems. It extends into Colorado and Utah. This unit of the NWRS is the result of a cooperative effort with the U.S. Bureau of Reclamation called the Upper Colorado River Basin Recovery Implementation Program. Our goal and program purposes are to accept

**REFUGE MAINTENANCE**

**LOWER KLAMATH NWR, CALIFORNIA**

The Service manages more than 500 National Wildlife Refuges across the United States and its Territories. Construction skills are often needed to build wildlife observation decks, trails, water control devices, and nesting structures.

USFWS/William Radke

conservation easement transfers from BOR for the protection of endangered fishes and fish and wildlife habitat by holding and managing easements as a part of the NWRS. Target fish include the Colorado squawfish, razorback sucker, humpback chub, and bonytail. Though most acquisitions for the Colorado River WMA will be through conservation easements, the Service may also protect habitat through cooperative agreements and fee title acquisitions. This refuge was established with the acquisition of 24 easement acres in Utah.

The Service established the Lost Trail National Wildlife Refuge in Flathead County, Montana. Acquisition of lands within this unit is part of an approved settlement between Interior, Montana Power Company, and the Confederated Salish and Kootenai Tribes as partial mitigation for habitat and wildlife losses associated with Kerr Dam. This area is part of Lost Trail Ranch which lies in a geographic drainage known as Pleasant Valley, through which Pleasant Valley Creek runs. Wetland habitats abound here, as the Ranch also encompasses the 160-acre Dahl Lake. Upland areas are a mosaic of prairie grasses, wildflowers, and coniferous and deciduous timbered areas. These habitats attract a wide variety of wildlife, ranging from redside shiners and Columbia River squawfish to grizzly bears and gray wolves. Eagles have an active nest next to Dahl Lake.

Navassa Island National Wildlife Refuge is an overlay refuge. The Service has a secondary interest in the island through a Memorandum of Understanding with the Office of Insular Affairs which holds primary jurisdiction. The island lies between Haiti and Jamaica. Two of the island's many plant and animal species that are of particular interest are the white-necked crow and the peregrine falcon. Its waters contain some of the most pristine and healthy coral reefs under United States jurisdiction.

We established Shawangunk Grasslands National Wildlife Refuge at the former Galeville Airport, an army training facility at Shawangunk, New York. This refuge contains some of the most significant grasslands in the Northeast. A diverse abundance of grassland species inhabit the refuge including breeding populations of bobolinks, savannah sparrows, grasshopper sparrows, and wintering populations of northern harriers and short-eared owls. The American Bird Conservancy designated the refuge as an Important Bird Area.

Whittlesey Creek National Wildlife Refuge in Bayfield County, Wisconsin, joined the NWRS in September. The refuge area includes Lake Superior coastal wetlands, sedge meadow, lowland hardwood swamp, black spruce swamp and other wetland types. Both Whittlesey and Terwilliger Creeks, classified by the Wisconsin Department of Natural Resources as Class A trout streams, run through the area and provide spawning grounds for native brook trout. Waterfowl, neotropical migrants, raptors, grassland birds, shorebirds, amphibians, as well as bald eagle, gray wolves and trumpeter swans use this area.

Through these new additions to the NWRS, the Service is committed to the preservation of biodiversity and the management of resources on an ecosystem basis. Land acquisition and balancing of NWRS and the NFHS resources are important tools used by the Service for attaining these goals.

*Condition of Stewardship Lands*

The Service has stewardship responsibilities for the lands and associated heritage assets under its jurisdiction, which are intertwined with the condition of the fish, wildlife and plant resources that depend on Service stewardship assets for their well-being and, in some cases, their survival. Service

National Fish Hatchery Employee
USFWS/Hollingsworth

FWS Employee with Wolf Pups
USFWS/George Gentry

and for migratory populations needing temporary stopover sites to rest, breed, feed, and to survive nationwide and, in some cases, worldwide seasonal migrations. While some individual units of stewardship lands can be improved at any time during their management cycles, the condition of the stewardship assets as a whole, protected by inclusion in both the NWRS and the NFHS, is sufficient to support the mission of the Service and the statutory purposes for which these conservation systems were authorized.

The Service assesses the condition of its stewardship lands and resources through monitoring habitat characteristics and determining whether management actions are needed to change those characteristics to benefit their usefulness to fish and wildlife resources. For example, the Service monitors habitat condition through assessment studies to determine habitat quality. Based on such studies, the Service may determine that specific management and protection actions are necessary. For example, sites may be restored to improve habitat for identified species or moist soils and wetlands may be managed to improve habitat productivity. New or different integrated pest management practices may be used to benefit stressed refuge resources or law enforcement actions may be increased to prevent potential or discovered illegal use of refuge resources. A wide variety of techniques, such as grazing, haying, prescribed burning, and farming, necessary to meet local and System resource management goals, may be used by the Service to promote the habitat characteristics necessary to benefit fish and wildlife resources throughout the NWRS and to meet the conservation goals of the Service. Thus, condition of stewardship lands managed by the Service is not in a static state. Land or habitat condition may be changing, either through the imposition of management techniques or through natural stressors or processes acting on those lands. It is the goal of the Service to provide habitat that optimizes the usefulness of stewardship lands to benefit fish and wildlife resources.

resources are managed or maintained in a state or condition so that fish and wildlife resources are conserved and protected for the continuing benefit of Americans and in a manner consistent with the requirements of conservation designations.

Stewardship lands managed by the Service include refuges, fish hatcheries, wilderness areas, National Natural Landmarks, Wild and Scenic Rivers, and other special designations and are used and managed in accordance with the explicit purposes of the statutes authorizing their acquisition or designation and directing their use and management. Lands placed in the land conservation systems managed by the Service are protected into perpetuity as long as they remain in the NWRS and the NFHS. As new acquisitions enter these conservation systems, lands are managed to maintain their natural state, to mitigate adverse effects of actions previously conducted by others, or to enhance existing conditions to improve benefits to fish and wildlife resources. The Service safeguards the stewardship values of the lands it administers through management actions taken on individual refuges and hatcheries; however, such actions are taken in consideration of the needs and purposes of entire conservation systems, the NWRS and the NFHS. The NWRS and the NFHS are conservation systems that provide integrated habitat and life support for both permanent resident populations

## HERITAGE ASSETS

Some of the Service's stewardship lands fall into the category of heritage assets. Heritage assets are those lands, buildings and structures, and associated resources recognized for their ecological, cultural, historical and scientific importance. Heritage assets also include cultural resources, such as archaeological resources and historic properties, and

USFWS/David E. Goeke

Sod House Ranch Barn Before Restoration
USFWS Photo

### Sod House Ranch - National Register of Historic Places

The Sod House Ranch, located on the Malheur National Wildlife Refuge, Oregon, was constructed in the late 1870's under the direction of Peter French. The ranch is listed in the National Register of Historic Places and is constructed of local materials including juniper and ponderosa pine. In the early 1990's, flooding from nearby Malheur Lake damaged the ranch's unique barn. In 1999, the Service completed a rehabilitation project of the barn in cooperation with the National Park Service, the State of Oregon's Division of Parks and Recreation, the University of Oregon Architectural School and the Northwest Youth Corps/ Americorps.

Restored Sod House Ranch Barn
USFWS Photo

museum collections derived from lands and facilities managed by the Service.

Heritage assets include those lands managed by the Service that carry overlay or special designations authorized by Congress, the President, the Secretary of the Interior or by conventions of national or international stature. Thus, heritage assets also include Wilderness Areas, Wild and Scenic Rivers, National Natural Landmarks, and Wetlands of International Importance. Such lands managed by the Service protect valuable natural and cultural resources in every State and a number of U.S. territories and possessions. The protection of these lands benefits not only the Nation's fish and wildlife populations, but helps preserve important elements of our past and cultural diversity. The condition of all

that have nationally recognized historical or cultural designations as heritage assets. Please refer to the Program Highlights section of this report for details on the deferred maintenance needs of all facilities managed by the Service. From this information, the Service concludes that the infrastructure that supports the mission work of the Service is suffering from accelerated deterioration. The overall condition of facilities managed by the Service, which includes heritage assets, is found to be in poor condition and in need of repair.

*Cultural Resources*

Lands managed by the Service are particularly important for protecting significant sites associated with the Nation's prehistory and history. By

Red Fox                                                    USFWS Photo

lands managed by the Service, including those lands represented by special designations of national or international importance, are discussed in previous paragraphs as well as in this section. Special designations are managed or maintained in a manner that preserves the values that originally qualified these assets for their special designations. The status and condition of cultural resources, museum collections, and facilities defined as heritage assets are discussed below.

*Condition of Heritage Asset Facilities*

Heritage assets are defined as property, plant and equipment of historical, natural, cultural, educational, or artistic significance. The Service defines those sites and facilities under its administration

closely examining their geographic distribution, an obvious pattern unfolds. Service lands are located along major river corridors, coastal areas, or in association with wetlands and North America's migratory bird flyways. These same areas have been used by humans for thousands of years for transportation, settlement, and subsistence. Archaeological and historic sites located on these lands contribute important information on changes to habitat and wildlife over time and offer fish and wildlife conservation partnership opportunities with local communities and tribes.

As of FY 1999, the Service documented over 11,000 archaeological and historic sites on a small percentage of its lands and estimates that it is responsible for tens of thousands of additional sites yet to be identified. Cultural properties range in age and type from the Sod House historic ranch on the Malheur NWR, Oregon to early 20th Century military fortifications in the Fort Dade on Egmont Key NWR, Florida to a 10,000 year old archaeological site on a refuge in Tennessee, to a segment of the Lewis and Clark National Historic Trail on the Charles M. Russell NWR, Montana, to the Victorian-era historic buildings on the D.C. Booth Historic Fish Hatchery in South Dakota. Cultural properties managed by the Service reflect our Nation's rich heritage and diversity.

Of the total number of known cultural resources, an estimated 99 sites or districts have been listed in the National Register of Historic Places, while an additional 409 are considered eligible for

Brown Bear                                    USFWS Photo

listing. The Service also manages 9 National Historic Landmarks designated by the Secretary of the Interior to protect and recognize sites of exceptional importance. Approximately 188 buildings and structures are considered eligible for listing in the National Register.

Inventories and records of archaeological and historic sites are maintained by each Service Regional Office for field stations under its jurisdiction. Service-wide information on the number and status of archaeological properties is summarized each year for the Secretary of the Interior's report to Congress required by the Archaeological Resources Protection Act.

The physical condition of cultural resources managed by the Service varies

tremendously, depending on location, maintenance, use, and type of resource. While no comprehensive assessment is available, the Service is developing guidance and criteria to begin collecting information. The Service estimates that a minimum of 10 years is required to assess the condition of identified cultural resources under its jurisdiction.

*Museum Collections*

Service museum collections consist of approximately 2.8 million objects maintained in 150 offices or on loan to over 200 non-Federal repositories for study and long-term care. Collections consist of archaeological materials excavated from Service managed cultural resources; paleontological collections; objects and documents associated with the agency's

history; wildlife art; and, wildlife, fisheries, and botanical specimens. Service collections are used for educational and interpretive programs, research on changes to habitat and wildlife, and maintaining the history and traditions of the Service's programs and employees.

In FY 1999, the Service's Northeast Region initiated an intensive program to catalog and protect important collections stored on field stations. One example is at the Chincoteague NWR in Virginia, which maintains an extensive historic waterfowl collection reflecting the by-gone era of unrestricted market hunting. As part of a program sponsored by the National Council for Preservation Education, the refuge hired a summer intern to conduct basic conservation work and catalog valuable waterfowl decoys, historic guns,

---

**Chincoteaque Historic Decoy Collection**

**Chincoteaque NWR, Virginia**

USFWS Photo

Wigeon - Artist: Miles Hancock, Chincoteaque, Virginia (1889-1975)

Miles Hancock made decoys for his own use in the 1920's and then began selling them to supplement his income. The carving and painting methods were of his own design. He is considered the last of the "old school" eastern shore decoy makers.

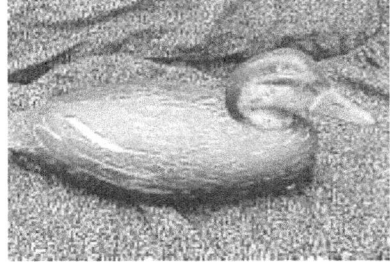

USFWS Photo

Black Duck - Artist: Ira Hudson, Chincoteaque, Virginia (1876-1949)

Ira Hudson, was Chincoteaque's most prolific decoy maker through the mid-20th century. Although he was an expert in waterfowl anatomy and imparted his knowledge on his gunning stools, he rarely picked up a shotgun.

*Wilderness is where the earth and its community of life are untrammeled by humans and where humans are visitors who do not remain.*

boats and other items. Information on each object in the collection was also entered into the Service's museum property software for tracking essential information.

The Service maintains a collection of artwork at the Academy of Natural Sciences of Philadelphia under a long-term loan agreement. The collection consists of 487 pieces of artwork created by notable painters such as Louis Agassiz Fuertes, Ernest Thompson Seton, and Jay Norwood (Ding) Darling. The artists were commissioned by the Bureau of Biological Survey, a predecessor to the Service, during the late 19th and early 20th centuries to depict various wildlife species and landscapes for use in government publications. Under the agreement, the Academy maintains the collection in a climate controlled and secure storage area to prevent deterioration and loss.

The Service continues to accession new museum collections each year, primarily

UL Bend Wildnerness Area Charles M. Russell NWR                    USFWS/Rick&Susie Graetz

as a result of the scientifically controlled excavation of archaeological sites on its lands. The overall condition of Service museum collections is adequate to good. Over 82 percent of the Service's collections are maintained on loan by museums and other institutions. The Service ensures that these collections are safeguarded through compliance with the Secretary of the Interior's curation standards found in 36 CFR 79. Institutions must maintain the appropriate environmental, record-keeping, and security controls in order to

qualify for maintaining Federal collections. Loan agreements signed by the Service and institutions create the basis for ensuring the perpetual care of these valuable materials.

Information standards for tracking the location, provenance or origin, and condition of museum collections are addressed by Service policy and data standards released in FY 1998. In an effort to assist field stations in managing their collections, the Service released a new museum property software package for tracking essential information and preparing annual reports. The Service estimates that it will require a minimum of ten years to account fully for its museum collections according to current standards.

*Special Designations*

The National Wilderness Preservation System was created by the Wilderness Protection Act of 1964. Designations ensure that lands in the Wilderness Preservation System are preserved and protected in their natural state. Wilderness is where the earth and its community of life are untrammeled by human beings and where humans themselves are visitors who do not remain. Of the approximately 104.8 million acres in the Wilderness Preservation System, the Service manages 75 wilderness areas encompassing 20.7 million acres in 26 States. This total represents approximately 20 percent of the National Wilderness Preservation System. These lands and resources are kept in their natural state and protected from man made disturbances and, as such, the condition of these lands are maintained so as to preserve the natural qualities for which they were originally designated. Although mostly located in the Western United States and Alaska, the Service manages a number of wilderness areas in the lower 48 States including two located on the Charles M. Russell NWR, Montana and the Mingo NWR, Missouri.

The Charles M. Russell NWR Wilderness Area encompasses 20,893 acres bordering a hairpin turn in the Missouri River, now part of Ft. Peck Reservoir. The area is rich in history, starting with a major Missouri River crossing for the vast bison herds as they moved north and south across central Montana. Native Americans followed the bison and signs of their presence are still evident. Later the Lewis and Clark expedition camped several days in the area, and it was a favorite resting spot when steamboats plied the Missouri. Vegetation is sagebrush grassland interspersed with juniper and chokecherry coulees. Wildlife is typical of the area and includes prairie songbirds and raptors, mule deer, elk, pronghorn, sharp-tailed and sage grouse. The wilderness is easily accessed via boat from Ft. Peck Reservoir and vistas are outstanding. On a clear day you can see over a hundred miles viewing landscapes often depicted by the famous western painter, Charley Russell.

The Mingo NWR Wilderness Area covers 7,730 acres of bottomland hardwood swamp formed in a linear basin of an ancient, abandoned channel of the Mississippi River and bordered by the foothills of the Ozark uplift. This wilderness area contains cypress and tupelo trees, American lotus, and hundreds of other species of trees and plants.

Information on wilderness areas is reported for each fiscal year in the Service's *Annual Report of Lands Under Control of the U.S. Fish and Wildlife Service.* Wilderness areas contribute significantly to the Service's primary mission and to the purposes for which the NWRS was authorized by helping to sustain healthy ecosystems and wildlife habitat.

For a river to be eligible for the National Wild and Scenic Rivers System, it must be in a free flowing condition and it must possess one or more specific value, such as scenic, recreational, geologic, fish and wildlife, historic, cultural, or other similarly unique characteristics worthy of preserving. Wild and Scenic eligibility studies are presented to Congress with a Presidential recommendation, where final designation is decided by Congress. There are 154 rivers containing 178 river segments included in the National Wild and Scenic River System and each mile designated is classified as either wild, scenic, or recreational. The total system encompasses approximately 10,931 river miles of which the Service manages segments of eight Wild and Scenic Rivers totaling approximately 1,258 miles in length. These rivers are destined to always run wild and free as long as they remain in the Wild and Scenic Rivers System and, as such, the condition of these lands and waters are maintained so as to preserve the natural qualities for which they were originally designated. For example, the Service manages the designated 80 mile segment of the Ivishak

Mingo Wilderness, Mingo NWR                                    USFWS Photo

River as part of the Arctic National Wildlife Refuge in Alaska. The Service and the National Park Service jointly manage designated segments of the Niobrara River, where the Service manages that part of the Niobara River that flows through the Ft. Niobrara National Wildlife Refuge in Nebraska.

National Natural Landmarks are management areas having national significance as sites that exemplify one of a natural region's characteristic biotic or geologic features. Sites must be one of the

Buffalo Grazing at Wichita Mountains NWR                    USFWS/Elise Smith

preserves the natural qualities for which they were originally designated. National Natural Landmarks are designated by the Secretary of the Interior because they possess characteristics of a particular type of natural feature, have not been seriously disturbed by humans, contain diverse or rare natural features, or possess outstanding scientific values and educational opportunities. For example, the Santa Ana NNL is considered to be a living museum of lowland forested areas along the Lower Rio Grande Valley, containing jungle-like vegetation and providing habitat for over 300 species of birds and some rare mammals.

Adopted in 1971, in Ramsar, Iran, the Convention on Wetlands of International Importance provides a framework for the conservation of wetlands worldwide. Marsh, fen, peatland, or water — static or flowing; fresh, brackish or salt — even riparian or coastal zones adjacent to wetlands are included in and protected by the Ramsar Convention, embraced by more than 100 nations throughout the world. Ramsar recognizes the special value of 775 Wetlands of International Importance located throughout 93 countries in the World. The U.S. demonstrated the importance it places on this convention by nominating its 16th and 17th sites this fiscal year – Sand Lake National Wildlife Refuge, South Dakota, and the Bolinas Lagoon, California. Sand Lake is the only Wetlands Convention site

best known examples of a unique feature and must be located in the United States or on the Continental Shelf. The more than 40 National Natural Landmarks, managed entirely or in part by the Service, contain important ecological or geological features deserving protection and further study. These areas, which encompass roughly 3.5 million acres, have been maintained relatively free of human disturbance for long periods of time and thus approximate a stable natural environment. This condition

*Lands and waters are managed by the FWS so that the natural qualities for which they were orginally designated are preserved.*

Alligator                                                  USFWS/George Gentry

Bird Tracking at Sand Lake NWR                    USFWS Photo

RAMSAR Plaque at Sand
Lake NWR        USFWS Photo

In the summer of 1997, Sand Lake NWR
began their journey to be listed as a
Wetland of International Importance.
They made land fall one year later,
becoming the 16th site in the U.S. and the
first site in the Prairie Pothole region to
receive such a distinction. On May 8, 1999,
the refuge and the Service employees who
are so dedicated to this special place were
honored.

Colonial nesting water birds abound on the
refuge. Sand Lake has the world's largest
nesting colony of Franklin Gulls. These
winged ambassadors are champion
migrators. The Gulls spend the winter in
Chile and Peru and return to North
American prairies to nest, a distance of
more than 12,000 miles. Through the
habitat it provides, Sand Lake NWR is
making a significant contribution to the
conservation of the world's wetlands.

within the Prairie Pothole Joint Venture
Area, a subdivision of the North American
Waterfowl Management Plan. Bolinas
Lagoon, managed by the Marin County
Open Space District, is a 1,100 acre tidal
embayment located as the south end of the
Point Reyes peninsula in California–the
first wetland to be nominated on the
Pacific Flyway in the lower 48 States. The
condition of these lands and waters are
maintained so as to preserve the natural
qualities for which they were originally
designated.

The Western Hemisphere Shorebird
Network (WHSRN) was created in 1986 to
foster international shorebird conservation
through partnerships among countries
throughout the Americas. Sites are
accepted into the WHSRN if they satisfy
biological criteria and all owners and
stakeholders agree to make a commitment
to shorebird conservation. The Service,
broadly supports the WHSRN. The
NWRS boasts an enormous array of
shorebird habitats. At present 19 sites are
managed within the NWRS, 7 of which
hold international status. Sites range
throughout the U.S. from Virginia's shores
(Eastern Shore NWR) to the California
coast (San Francisco Bay NWR). Several
refuges are scheduled to become WHSRN
sites in FY 2000.

CCC Worker banding a Franklin's Gull (1937)                    USFWS Photo

# Financial Statements

*Overview of Financial Results of Service Operations*

In accordance with the Chief Financial Officers Act of 1990, the Service annually prepares financial statements of position. Accordingly, the following financial statements display the financial position and net cost of operations for the Service during FY 1999.

*Analysis of Revenues and Financing Sources*

In FY 1999, the Service's total financing sources amounted to $1.720 billion, which is approximately a 21% increase from the FY 1998 level. The primary financing source for the Service is Congressional appropriations. Appropriated funding supports the Service's core natural resource programs, such as endangered species and habitat conservation, and operations and maintenance for National Wildlife Refuges and National Fish Hatcheries. In FY 1999, the Service's appropriations from the Congress increased by 5% from the FY 1998 level of $1.384 billion to $1.454 billion.

The second significant category of revenue that the Service utilizes is non-exchange revenue. The use of these revenues is restricted for specific purposes by statutes authorizing the revenue source. Therefore, these funds are not used for general operations. Among the types of non-exchange revenues the Service receives are receipts from excise taxes relating to migratory bird hunting activities and interest earned from investments of excise taxes on firearms and ammunition. The Service collects fines and penalties levied by the courts on those apprehended in the illegal possession or trafficking of fish, wildlife and plants. Additionally, the Service is authorized to receive monetary contributions to fund conservation activities. In FY 1999, the Service's non-exchange revenue increased significantly from $104 million to $313 million. The majority of this increase, $210 million, was attributed to changes in the accounting classification of certain excise taxes. Other major changes include a $ million increase in fines and permit fees relating to the Migratory Bird Conservation Act, $

million in budgetary transfers for land acquisition and infrastructure maintenance projects, and a $ million transfer providing emergency funding for computer hardware and software upgrades in preparation for the Year 2000.

*Deferred Maintenance on Facilities*

In order to understand the condition of Service facilities, the Service estimates deferred maintenance needs for the facilities and infrastructure that support the mission work of the Service. Annually, the Service must defer needed maintenance because of inadequately funded maintenance due to insufficient budgets, growth of the infrastructure without commensurate operations and maintenance funding and competition for resources from other management needs. Having to defer repairs, rehabilitation or replacement of facilities and the physical resources fixed to facilities leads to accelerated facility deterioration. Such deterioration of facilities can adversely impact public and employee health and safety, disrupt operations of the Service, and compromise the conservation of fish and wildlife resources.

In this report, the Service discloses a future liability estimated at approximately $930 million, plus or minus 15%, placing our estimate within a range between $790 million to $1.1 billion for deferred maintenance in both the National Wildlife Refuge and the National Fish Hatchery Systems. The estimate for FY 1999 is greater than our estimate as of the end of FY 1998, which was approximately $750 million, plus or minus 15%. These two systems, individually and in the aggregate are in poor condition, as measured by the Facility Condition Index, which is a commonly used industry measurement of facility condition. The average estimate within the range indicates that a one-time funding initiative of approximately $930 million would be required to raise the condition of Service operating assets from poor to good. Based on the replacement estimates for existing facilities, the Service would require an annual maintenance budget higher than current or projected levels to maintain these assets in fair or good condition.

The replacement values for the NFHS infrastructure ($800 million) and for the NWRS infrastructure ($4.5 billion) are undergoing internal review by the Service. Replacement values for NFHS resources were originally estimated in 1992. Since the figure has been revised periodically over the past six years based on inflation and the Consumer Price Index, the NFHS is in the process of updating and verifying this estimate to make it current. Replacement values for NWRS resources are historical estimates originating over 15 years ago and revised periodically based on substantial growth of the NWRS and inflation and are the best available data by which to assess the aggregate condition of NWRS resources. Using these figures, the Service estimates the total replacement value of Service operating assets to be at approximately $5.3 billion. Private sector or industry standards suggest that no less than 2% to 4% of the total replacement value of the asset should be expended annually for proper maintenance. Under this guideline, the Service would require an annual maintenance budget of at least $106 million in order to properly maintain the existing infrastructure of the NWRS and the NFHS. New additions to Service infrastructure will require commensurate increases to the maintenance budget of the Service to prevent increases in deferred maintenance.

Currently, Service maintenance budgets are increasing, but are still less than half of the annual estimated needs to assure that Service operating assets are maintained properly. We estimate that existing Service infrastructure, under accelerated deterioration, will remain in poor condition without significant budgetary resources to improve their condition. As a result of not receiving sufficient operations and maintenance funding, the Service, by default, may consider either closing facilities or reducing public access to these resources, neither of which is a desirable management action by the Service. The Service has established a priority goal in its newly revised 5-Year Strategic Plan to complete its evaluation of replacement values for NWRS infrastructure by FY 2000, which will help the Service meet its conservative goals for infrastructure improvements by FY 2003. When met, these conservative goals may help the Service raise the condition of its operating assets from poor to fair.

*Equipment Replacement and Repair*

Although the estimates for deferred maintenance exclude associated equipment, the Service is tracking equipment needs in much the same manner as facility condition and maintenance. Equipment includes replacement or repair of "non-fixed" or portable physical resources (e.g., heavy equipment, transportation equipment and vehicles, small portable tools, computers and office equipment, and shop, lab, security, communications or other operational equipment). The equipment that the Service tracks are those that need repair, rehabilitation, or replacement to bring them up to acceptable operating condition necessary for the Service to complete its mission and to conserve resources for which the Service has stewardship responsibility. The Service has determined that much of its equipment is in poor condition and, thus, in need of repair, rehabilitation or replacement.

Estimating the equipment backlog for the NWRS and the NFHS requires specifying equipment parameters and seeking competitive prices among differing vendors. As such, estimates may vary by 10% above or below the discrete number provided. However, the Service uses the median number within the range as the best estimate of the existing equipment backlog. The median estimate for the equipment backlog for the NWRS is approximately $158 million and for the NFHS is approximately $19 million, with a combined total of approximately $177 million. As a result of this liability on average, a one-time funding initiative of $177 million would be required to raise the condition of Service operating equipment assets from poor to an acceptable operating condition. Based on historical trends in annual maintenance budgets, the Service would require higher than current projected funds to maintain these assets in operating condition. The equipment backlog is an estimate of replacement cost. Private sector or industry standards suggest that no less than 2% to 4% of the total replacement value of the asset should be expended annually for proper maintenance. Under this guideline, the Service would require an annual equipment maintenance budget of at least $3.5 million in order to properly maintain equipment managed by the Service. New additions to Service infrastructure and staff will require commensurate increases to the maintenance budget of the Service to prevent increases to the equipment replacement and repair backlog.

*Environmental Contaminant Liabilities*

In the Footnote to the Financial Statements estimating environmental contaminant liabilities, the Service does not include the costs of restoring stewardship values or fish and wildlife resources that are degraded by offsite activities beyond the control of the Service. This determination is required by Technical Release No. 2 of the Accounting and Auditing Policy Committee (AAPC) established to interpret FASAB Standards.

As a result, the Service may have additional future costs associated with restoring stewardship values or fish and wildlife resources that are not estimated or disclosed in this report. Although the Service has legal means by which to seek compensation from polluters for damages to natural resources resulting from exposure to such contaminants, such legal proceedings are costly and time consuming for the Service and for other affected land and resource managers, such as State and local governments. A connection between the polluter as a source of the discovered contaminant and damage to the natural resource from that pollutant must be proven, the damages assessed and quantified, and technical data presented through courts. Also, most cases pursued under such proceedings are usually settled out of court, resulting in an award from the court that is less than the estimated value of the damages to fish and wildlife resources, resulting in restoration that does not fully compensate the American public for lost or damaged natural resources in affected units of the NWRS and the NFHS.

The Service seeks compensation from polluters who contribute to contamination of Service lands and waters and does so where responsible parties are clearly identified. In many cases, responsible parties cannot be clearly identified among many possible sources or cannot be found or are no longer a financially viable entity. In these instances, the Service uses its appropriated funds to remove contaminants before they can adversely affect the health and welfare of fish and wildlife resources and people. The Service dedicates approximately $2 million annually to cleaning up contaminants found on units of the NWRS, which are usually discovered after acquisition, left as residual after transfer from other agencies, or have their origins off Service lands. Inability to identify and recover costs from responsible parties represents a potential future diversion of Service funds from planned activities and potential costs to the American public.

*Year 2000 Readiness*

To ensure all computers and information systems are ready for the Year 2000, the Service participated with the Department of the Interior in a Department-wide initiative to analyze and correct potential Year 2000 conflicts. Mission critical systems in the Service were certified through independent validation and verification as Year 2000 compliant and mission essential Service facilities were tested and certified. A discussion of the Department's state of readiness, the costs of addressing Year 2000 issues, the risks to the Department of Year 2000 issues, and the Department's contingency plan is presented in management's discussion and analysis included in the Department of the Interior's Fiscal Year 1999 Accountability Report.

**U.S. FISH AND WILDLIFE SERVICE**
**BALANCE SHEET**
**AS OF SEPTEMBER 30, 1999**
**(DOLLARS IN THOUSANDS)**

## ASSETS

*Service Assets*

| | | |
|---|---|---|
| Fund Balance with Treasury (Note 2) | $ | 895,533 |
| Cash (Note 3) | | 603 |
| Investments (Note 4) | | 426,361 |
| Accounts Receivable, Net (Note 5) | | |
|     With the Public | | 5,292 |
|     Due from Federal Agencies | | 416,855 |
| Forfeited Property (Note 7) | | 5,027 |
| Property, Plant, and Equipment, Net (Note 6) | | 758,007 |
| Interest Receivable (Note 5) | | |
|     Due from Federal Agencies | | 61 |
| Advances | | 582 |
|     Total Service Assets | | 2,508,321 |

*Assets Held on Behalf of Others*

| | | |
|---|---|---|
| Interest Receivable (Note 5) | | |
|     With the Public | | 115 |
|     Total Assets Held on Behalf of Others | | 115 |
| **TOTAL ASSETS** | $ | 2,508,436 |

*The accompanying notes are an integral part of this financial statement.*

**U.S. FISH AND WILDLIFE SERVICE**
**BALANCE SHEET**
**AS OF SEPTEMBER 30, 1999**
**(DOLLARS IN THOUSANDS)**

## LIABILITIES

*Liabilities Covered by Budgetary Resources*

Accounts Payable (Note 8)
| | | |
|---|---|---|
| With the Public.................................................................................... | $ | 35,539 |
| Due to Federal Agencies.................................................................... | | 9,723 |

Other Liabilities (Note 8)
| | |
|---|---|
| With the Public.................................................................................... | 21,277 |
| Due to Federal Agencies.................................................................... | 83,831 |

Total Liabilities Covered by Budgetary Resources................................. 150,370

*Liabilities Not Covered by Budgetary Resources*

Other Liabilities (Note 8)
| | |
|---|---|
| With the Public.................................................................................... | 33,435 |
| Due to Federal Agencies.................................................................... | 8,825 |
| Environmental Contaminant and Contingent Liabilities (Note 8)............... | 42,000 |
| Other Actuarial Liabilities (Note 8)......................................................... | 38,408 |

Total Liabilities Not Covered by Budgetary Resources............................. 122,668

**TOTAL LIABILITIES................................................................................** 273,038

## NET POSITION

| | |
|---|---|
| Unexpended Appropriations (Note 9)......................................................... | 1,104,814 |
| Cumulative Results of Operations.............................................................. | 1,130,584 |

**TOTAL NET POSITION..........................................................................** 2,235,398

**TOTAL LIABILITIES AND NET POSITION.................................................** $ 2,508,436

*The accompanying notes are an integral part of this financial statement.*

## U.S. FISH AND WILDLIFE SERVICE
## CONSOLIDATED STATEMENT OF NET COST
## FOR THE YEAR ENDED SEPTEMBER 30, 1999
## (DOLLARS IN THOUSANDS)

| | Sustainability of Fish and Wildlife Populations | Habitat Conservation: A Network of of Lands and Water | Public Use and Enjoyment | Consolidated Total |
|---|---|---|---|---|
| **PROGRAM EXPENSES:** | | | | |
| Operating Expenses | | | | |
| With Federal Agencies | $ 83,888 | $ 106,237 | $ 37,030 | $ 227,155 |
| With the Public | 411,499 | 707,887 | 124,615 | 1,244,001 |
| Total Operating Expenses | 495,387 | 814,124 | 161,645 | 1,471,156 |
| Interest Expense | | | | |
| With the Public | 17 | 47 | 6 | 70 |
| Total Interest Expense | 17 | 47 | 6 | 70 |
| Depreciation and Amortization | 14,686 | 16,192 | 6,778 | 37,656 |
| Bad Debt Expense | 295 | 49 | 8 | 352 |
| Imputed Costs | 12,788 | 14,099 | 5,902 | 32,789 |
| Expenses Not Requiring Budgetary Resources | (35,396) | (39,026) | (16,337) | (90,759) |
| Other Expenses | 198 | 218 | 91 | 507 |
| Total Program Expenses | 487,975 | 805,703 | 158,093 | 1,451,771 |
| **PROGRAM REVENUES:** | | | | |
| Sale of Goods and Services to Federal Agencies | (27,987) | (85,018) | (9,048) | (122,053) |
| Sale of Goods and Services to the Public | (11,415) | (27,676) | (3,321) | (42,412) |
| Total Program Revenues | (39,402) | (112,694) | (12,369) | (164,465) |
| **NET COST OF OPERATIONS** | $ 448,573 | $ 693,009 | $ 145,724 | $ 1,287,306 |

*The accompanying notes are an integral part of this financial statement.*

**U.S. FISH AND WILDLIFE SERVICE**
**CONSOLIDATED STATEMENT OF CHANGES IN NET POSITION**
**FOR THE YEAR ENDED SEPTEMBER 30, 1999**
**(DOLLARS IN THOUSANDS)**

| | | |
|---|---|---:|
| NET COST OF OPERATIONS.................................................................. | $ | (1,287,306) |
| **FINANCING SOURCES** | | |
| **(Other than Exchange Revenues):** | | |
| Appropriations Used................................................................. | | 1,454,419 |
| Other Revenue Transfers........................................................... | | 307,330 |
| Donations............................................................................... | | 6,126 |
| Imputed Financing (Note 10)..................................................... | | 32,789 |
| Net Transfers.......................................................................... | | (80,216) |
| NET RESULTS OF OPERATIONS............................................................. | | 433,142 |
| PRIOR PERIOD ADJUSTMENTS (Note 11)................................................ | | (82,053) |
| NET CHANGE IN CUMULATIVE RESULTS OF OPERATIONS............................ | | 351,089 |
| INCREASE (DECREASE) IN UNEXPENDED APPROPRIATIONS......................... | | (165,141) |
| CHANGE IN NET POSITION.................................................................. | | 185,948 |
| NET POSITION - BEGINNING OF PERIOD................................................. | | 2,049,450 |
| **NET POSITION - END OF PERIOD**........................................................ | $ | 2,235,398 |

*The accompanying notes are an integral part of this financial statement.*

**U.S. FISH AND WILDLIFE SERVICE**
**CONSOLIDATED STATEMENT OF BUDGETARY RESOURCES**
**FOR THE YEAR ENDED SEPTEMBER 30, 1999**
**(DOLLARS IN THOUSANDS)**

| | Operating Funds | Special Receipt Funds | Trust Funds | Consolidated Total |
|---|---|---|---|---|
| **BUDGETARY RESOURCES** | | | | |
| Budget Authority............................................. $ | 836,737 | $ 386,966 | $ 274,812 | $ 1,498,515 |
| Unobligated Balance - Beginning of Period............. | 223,354 | 323,951 | 121,783 | 669,088 |
| Unobligated Balance - Transfers........................... | 1,483 | 16,900 | - | 18,383 |
| Spending Authority From Offsetting Collections...... | 128,931 | 72,731 | - | 201,662 |
| Downward Adjustments of Prior Year Obligations.... | 23,033 | 33,933 | 31,353 | 88,319 |
| Total Budgetary Resources................................. $ | 1,213,538 | $ 834,481 | $ 427,948 | $ 2,475,967 |
| | | | | |
| **STATUS OF BUDGETARY RESOURCES** | | | | |
| Obligations Incurred......................................... $ | 972,183 | $ 446,655 | $ 315,688 | $ 1,734,526 |
| Unobligated Balance, Available - End of Period........ | 228,036 | 387,826 | 112,260 | 728,122 |
| Unobligated Balance, Not Available - End of Period.. | 13,319 | - | - | 13,319 |
| Total, Status of Budgetary Resources.................... $ | 1,213,538 | $ 834,481 | $ 427,948 | $ 2,475,967 |
| | | | | |
| **OUTLAYS** | | | | |
| Obligations Incurred......................................... $ | 972,183 | $ 446,655 | $ 315,688 | $ 1,734,526 |
| Less: | | | | |
|    Spending Authority From Offsetting Collections... | 128,931 | 72,731 | - | 201,662 |
|    Downward Adjustments of Prior Year Obligations. | 23,033 | 33,933 | 31,353 | 88,319 |
| Obligated Balance, Net - Beginning of Period.......... | 200,165 | 262,508 | 266,570 | 729,243 |
| Less: | | | | |
|    Obligated Balance, Net - End of Period.............. | 243,427 | 265,394 | 286,702 | 795,523 |
| Total Outlays................................................. $ | 776,957 | $ 337,105 | $ 264,203 | $ 1,378,265 |

*The accompanying notes are an integral part of this financial statement.*

**U.S. FISH AND WILDLIFE SERVICE**
**CONSOLIDATED STATEMENT OF FINANCING**
**FOR THE YEAR ENDED SEPTEMBER 30, 1999**
**(DOLLARS IN THOUSANDS)**

## OBLIGATIONS AND NONBUDGETARY RESOURCES

| | |
|---|---:|
| Obligations incurred.................................................................................................... $ | 1,734,526 |
| Less: | |
| Spending authority for offsetting collectionsand adjustments..................................................... | (293,129) |
| Donations not in the budget............................................................................................ | 428 |
| Imputed financing source............................................................................................... | 32,789 |
| Transfers-in (out)....................................................................................................... | 5,436 |
| Exchange revenue not in the budget.................................................................................. | (80,116) |
| Non-exchange revenue not in the budget............................................................................ | 10,812 |
| Other financing sources................................................................................................ | 34,472 |
| Total Obligations and Nonbudgetary Resources, as Adjusted....................................... | 1,445,218 |

## RESOURCES THAT DO NOT FUND NET COST OF OPERATIONS

| | |
|---|---:|
| Change in amount of goods, services, and benefits ordered | |
| but not yet received or provided .................................................................................. | 11,765 |
| Costs capitalized on the balance sheet ............................................................................. | (48,114) |
| Total Resources That Do Not Fund Net Cost of Operations............................................ | (36,349) |

## COSTS THAT DO NOT REQUIRE RESOURCES

| | |
|---|---:|
| Depreciation and amortization......................................................................................... | 37,656 |
| Prior period adjustments............................................................................................... | (68,054) |
| Loss on disposition of assets.......................................................................................... | (507) |
| Other...................................................................................................................... | (12) |
| Total Costs That Do Not Require Resources....................................................... | (30,917) |

## FINANCING SOURCES YET TO BE PROVIDED.................................................... (90,646)

## NET COST OF OPERATIONS.................................................................. $ 1,287,306

*The accompanying notes are an integral part of this financial statement.*

# Notes to Prinicipal Financial Statements

## NOTE 1.  SUMMARY OF SIGNIFICANT ACCOUNTING POLICIES

### A. Basis of Presentation

These financial statements have been prepared to report the financial position and results of operations of the U.S. Fish and Wildlife Service (Service) as required by the Chief Financial Officers Act of 1990. They have been prepared from the books and records of the Service in conformity with generally accepted accounting principles (GAAP). Although a common data source is used, these statements are different from those used to monitor and control budgetary resources. These statements should be read with the realization that they are for a sovereign entity, that unfunded liabilities reported in the financial statements cannot be liquidated without the enactment of an appropriation, and that the payment of all non-contract liabilities can be abrogated by the Government acting in its sovereign capacity.

### B. Reporting Entity

The Service is responsible for conserving, protecting, and enhancing fish and wildlife and their habitats for the continuing benefit of the American people.

Authority over money, or other budget authority made available to the Service, is vested in the Director of the Service. The Director is responsible for administrative oversight and policy direction of the Service. Accounts are maintained which restrict the use of money (or other budget authority) to the purposes and time-period for which authorized. These accounts also provide assurance that obligations do not exceed authorized amounts.

The accompanying financial statements have been prepared from the Service's consolidated standard general ledger. The statements include are all funds and accounts under the control of the Service as well as allocations from other Federal agency appropriations transferred to the Service under specific legislative authority. The Service is responsible for maintaining accounts in multiple funds. Overall, there are five separate fund types:

1. *General Funds* -- These funds are expenditure accounts used to record financial transactions arising from congressional appropriations or other authorizations to spend general revenues. The principal general funds are:

a.  Resource Management
b.  Construction
c.  Cooperative Endangered Species Conservation
d.  National Wildlife Refuge Fund
e.  North American Wetlands Conservation Fund
f.  Wildlife Conservation and Appreciation Fund
g.  Multi-National Species Fund

2. *Trust Funds* -- The Service maintains two trust fund accounts to carry out specific programs under trust agreements and statutes. (1) The Sport Fish Restoration Account makes grants available to States for support projects that restore, conserve, manage, protect, and enhance sport fish resources and coastal wetlands and projects that provide for public use and benefits from sport fish resources. The Service's Sport Fish Restoration Account derives benefits from the Aquatic Resources Trust Fund maintained by the U.S. Department of the Treasury (Treasury) which collects and invests those funds. The Appropriations Act of 1951 authorized amounts equal to revenues credited during the year to be used in the subsequent fiscal year. This is recorded as permanent appropriations to remain available until expended. These statements do not reflect the amounts collected and held by the Treasury in this fiscal year for reporting in subsequent years. (2) The Contributed Fund trust fund receives contributions for projects relating to endangered species recovery, refuge operation and maintenance, research, and others.

3. *Deposit Funds* -- These funds are maintained to account for receipts awaiting proper classification. Proceeds from the sale of vehicles are also included in these funds.

4. *Receipt Funds* -- These funds arise from the sovereign and regulatory powers unique to the Government. These funds include miscellaneous fines and penalties, administrative fees, interest, and unclaimed monies.

5. *Special Funds* -- Collections made into special fund receipt accounts are earmarked by law for a specific purpose, but are not generated from a continuing cycle of operations. Most of these receipts are available immediately. Special fund expenditure accounts record amounts appropriated from special fund receipts, which are used for special programs, as specified by law. The principal special funds are:

a.  Land Acquisition (subject to appropriation)
b.  Federal Aid/Wildlife Restoration
c.  Operation/Maintenance - Quarters
d.  Proceeds from Sales - Water Resources Development        Projects
e.  Migratory Bird Conservation
f.  Federal Aid/Fish Restoration
g.  North American Wetlands Conservation
h.  National Wildlife Refuge
i.  Cooperative Endangered Species Conservation (subject to appropriation)
j.  Recreational Fee Demonstration Program
k.  Lahontan Valley and Pyramid Lake Fish and Wildlife Fund

### C. Basis of Accounting

Transactions are recorded on both an accrual accounting basis and a budgetary basis. Under the accrual method, revenues are recognized when earned and expenses are recognized when a liability is incurred, without regard to receipt or payment of cash. Budgetary accounting facilitates compliance with legal constraints and controls over the use of Federal funds.

### D. Revenues and Other Financing Sources

The Service receives the majority of the funding needed to support its programs through appropriations. The Service receives annual, multi-year, and no-year appropriations that may be used within statutory limits for operating expenses and capital expenditures (primarily equipment, furniture, and furnishings). Additional amounts are obtained through reimbursements for services provided to public entities and other Federal agencies.

Receipts are recognized as revenues when earned. These revenues may be used to offset the cost of operations at field sites, including overhead costs.

### E. Funds with Treasury and Cash

Cash receipts and disbursements are processed by Treasury. The balance with Treasury represents all unexpended balances in Service accounts. The funds with Treasury and cash include appropriated and trust funds, which are available to pay current liabilities and to pay outstanding obligations.

### F. Allowance for Doubtful Accounts

An Allowance for Doubtful Accounts is maintained to reflect uncollectible accounts receivable due from the public. The allowance amount is determined based on an average of prior year write-offs and an analysis of outstanding accounts receivable.

### G. Investments in U.S. Government Securities

Investments in U.S. Government securities are reported at amortized cost. Discounts are amortized into interest income over the term of the investment. Premiums are amortized against semi-annual interest receipts. It is the intent of the Service to hold investments to maturity. No provision is made for unrealized gains or losses on these securities.

### H. Operating Materials and Supplies

Operating materials and supplies consist of items such as lumber, sand, gravel, and other items purchased in large quantities which will be consumed in future operations. Operating materials and supplies are accounted for based on the purchases method. Under this method, operating materials and supplies are expensed when purchased.

### I. Land, Property, Plant, and Equipment

The Service defines capitalized equipment as those assets, other than buildings or other structures, which have an estimated useful life of greater than 1 year and an initial acquisition cost exceeding $25,000. Depreciation is recorded using the straight-line method based on the estimated useful life of the respective assets of no more than 10 years.

Capitalized buildings and structures have a cumulative cost of $50,000 or more. Buildings are comprised of service facilities, such as houses, garages, shops, schools, laboratories, and other buildings owned by the Service. Structures and facilities are comprised of service facilities,

such as powerhouses and pumping plants, structural and general service facilities systems (drainage system, plumbing system, sewer system, ventilating system, water system, heating system, etc.,), grounds and site improvements (roads and roadways, fences, lawns, shrubbery, parking areas, sidewalks, sprinkler systems, yard drainage systems, yard lighting systems, etc.,), bridges and trestles, dams and dikes, waterways, wells, etc., owned by the Service.

These buildings and structures are used in the operations of wildlife refuges, fish hatcheries, wildlife research centers, fishery research stations, waterfowl production areas, and administrative sites. Capitalized costs include materials, labor, and overhead costs incurred during construction and fees such as attorney and architect and building permits. Depreciation is recorded using the straight-line method based on an estimated useful life of 30 years.

Property is reported in the financial statements based upon legal ownership.

Consistent with the accounting standards for property, plant, and equipment, most lands under the control of the Service are classified as stewardship land and are reported on a separate Supplementary Stewardship Report. However, lands associated with administrative sites are reported on the Balance Sheet.

### J. Seized and Forfeited Property

The Service is responsible for safeguarding seized and forfeited property, from the time of seizure through the final disposition of the property. Disposition may include forfeiting the property to the Government, returning the property to the person from whom seized, destruction, sale, donation, or other methods authorized by law. Property for which a legal market exists is reported at appraised value.

Certain types of property may not be legally sold under Service regulations. Such property includes items that consists in whole or in part of migratory birds, bald and golden eagles, endangered or threatened species, marine mammals, and species listed on Appendix I to the Convention on International Trade in Endangered Species to Wild Fauna and Flora. Such property is classified as "Non-Marketable" and has no legal value.

### K. Contingencies

Contingent liabilities are recognized based upon the probability of occurrence. Administrative proceedings, legal actions, and pending claims are recognized in the accounting records when the event which may result in a liability is considered probable and may have a material impact upon the operations of the Service.

### L. Liabilities

Liabilities represent the amount of monies or other resources that are likely to be paid by the Service as the result of a transaction or event that has already occurred. However, without an appropriation, the Service cannot pay a liability. Liabilities for which an appropriation has not been enacted are therefore classified as unfunded liabilities. There is no certainty that the appropriations will be enacted. The Government, acting in its sovereign capacity, can abrogate non-contract liabilities of the Service.

### M. Annual, Sick, and Other Leave

Annual leave is accrued as it is earned. This accrual is reduced as leave is taken. Each year, the balance in the accrued annual leave account is adjusted to reflect current pay rates. To the extent current or prior year appropriations are not available to fund annual leave, future financing sources will be used.

Sick leave and other types of nonvested leave are expensed as taken because they are nonvesting in nature.

### N. Retirement Plans

Service employees contribute to the Civil Service Retirement System (CSRS) or the Federal Employees' Retirement System (FERS), to which the Service makes matching contributions.

Employees hired after December 31, 1983, are automatically covered by FERS. Employees hired prior to January 1, 1984, could elect either FERS or CSRS coverage. FERS offers a savings plan to which the Service automatically contributes 1 percent of pay and matches employee contributions up to an additional 4 percent of basic pay. For most FERS employees, the Service also contributes the employer's matching share for Social Security.

*O. Supplemental Schedules*

Supplemental schedules are presented after these notes for clarification and further disclosure.

## NOTE 2. FUND BALANCE WITH TREASURY

Cash receipts and disbursements are processed by Treasury. The fund balance with Treasury represents all unexpended balances in Service accounts and the right to draw on the Treasury for allowable expenditures. The fund balances with Treasury as of September 30, 1999 are comprised of the following amounts (dollars in thousands):

| | | |
|---|---|---:|
| **Service Assets:** | | |
| Operating Funds | $ | 485,029 |
| Special Receipt Funds | | 229,445 |
| Unavailable Receipt Funds | | 166,226 |
| Trust Funds | | 14,833 |
| Total Service Assets | | 895,533 |
| **Total Fund Balance** | $ | 895,533 |

## NOTE 3. CASH

Entity cash consists of $603,088 in petty cash imprest funds.

## NOTE 4. INVESTMENTS

Investments in non-marketable market-based U.S. Government securities consist of one bill purchased through the Bureau of Public Debt of Treasury. The invested funds consist of excise tax receipts from 14X5029, the Federal Aid in Wildlife Restoration fund. Amortization is recorded using the straight-line method. Outstanding investments in U.S. Government securities as of September 30, 1999 totaled (dollars in thousands):

| | Acquisition Cost | | Unamortized Premium/ (Discount) | | Net Investments | |
|---|---|---:|---|---:|---|---:|
| 14X5029 | $ | 426,361 | $ | - | $ | 426,361 |
| | $ | 426,361 | $ | - | $ | 426,361 |

## NOTE 5. ACCOUNTS RECEIVABLE AND INTEREST RECEIVABLE

Accounts and interest receivable consist of amounts owed the Service by other Federal agencies and amounts owed by the public. Accounts and interest receivable as of September 30, 1999 consist of (dollars in thousands):

| | Service Receivables | | Receivables Held on Behalf of Others | |
| --- | --- | --- | --- | --- |
| | Intragovernmental | With the Public | Intragovernmental | With the Public |
| Accounts Receivable | $ 416,855 | $ 5,292 | $ 0 | $ 0 |
| Interest Receivable | 61 | 0 | 0 | 115 |
| Total | $ 416,916 | $ 5,292 | $ 0 | $ 115 |

## NOTE 6. PROPERTY, PLANT, AND EQUIPMENT

Property, plant, and equipment as of September 30, 1999 consist of the following (dollars in thousands):

| | Service Life | Acquisition Value | Accumulated Depreciation | Net Book Value |
| --- | --- | --- | --- | --- |
| Land | | $ 10,493 | $ 0 | $ 10,493 |
| Buildings | 30 years | 416,303 | 141,044 | 275,259 |
| Other Structures | 30 years | 505,107 | 233,373 | 271,734 |
| Equipment | NTE 10 years | 163,778 | 95,223 | 68,555 |
| Subtotal PP&E | | 1,085,188 | 469,640 | 615,548 |
| Construction in Progress | | 131,966 | 0 | 131,966 |
| Total | | $ 1,227,647 | $ 469,640 | $ 758,007 |

## NOTE 7.  SEIZED AND FORFEITED PROPERTY

Property seized by the Service typically includes wildlife and wildlife products.  Seized and forfeited property as of September 30, 1999 consist of the following (number of seizures in thousands and dollars in thousands):

| | | Marketable | |
| --- | --- | --- | --- |
| | # of Seizures | | Value |
| Seized Property | 9 | $ | 1,056 |
| Forfeited Property | 124 | $ | 5,027 |
| Property Dispositions | 820 | $ | 1,827 |

## NOTE 8.  OTHER LIABILITIES

*A.  Other Liabilities Covered by Budgetary Resources*

All other liabilities covered by budgetary resources are current liabilities.

Advances are related to reimbursable agreements with public entities and other Federal agencies to protect wildlife resources, to conduct investigations, to conduct wildlife surveys on public lands, and to provide fish migration prior to the construction of new dams.

Deposit funds include stale-dated Government checks (of 1 year or greater), proceeds from the sale of vehicles not applied toward the purchase of new vehicles, and tax withholding.

The unearned revenue relates to property forfeited to the Service.

Other liabilities with the public are an offset to revenue collected for Treasury, which will be returned to the Treasury as required by new procedures for accounting for miscellaneous receipts.  Other liabilities covered by budgetary resources as of September 30, 1999 consist of the following (dollars in thousands):

| | Liabilities Covered by Budgetary Resources | | |
| --- | --- | --- | --- |
| | Intragovernmental | | With the Public |
| Accounts Payable | $ 9,723 | $ | 35,539 |
| Accrued Payroll/Benefits | 4,544 | | 17,946 |
| Advances | 16,755 | | 548 |
| Unearned Revenue | 62,532 | | 2,641 |
| Other | 0 | | 142 |
| Total Other Liabilities Covered by Budgetary Resources | $ 93,554 | $ | 56,816 |

Other liabilities not covered by budgetary resources total $33.4 million which represent the accrued unfunded annual leave of the Service, $8.8 million for unfunded workman's compensation accrual of the Service, and $38.4 million for the Federal Employees Compensation Act (FECA) actuarial calculation.

Environmental liabilities for the Service are associated with the future costs of remediating hazardous wastes and existing landfills existing within units of the National Wildlife Refuge System and on National Fish Hatcheries. The Service believes that the future costs of cleaning certain contamination within the NWRS and NFHS can be reasonably estimated at approximately $42 million. This estimate of future costs covers cleanup of 9 sites and include sites on lands obtained by the Service through donation, acquisition, or transfer from other agencies. Cost estimates are based on preliminary investigation of known sites and the expected degree and type of contamination probable at these sites. It does not include sites unknown, sites for which Service responsibility is unclear, sites which have not been investigated, or sites degraded by offsite activities beyond the control of the Service. Where possible, cost estimates are included for conducting site investigations and for conducting monitoring actions needed to assess the efficacy of cleanup. The Service's methods for estimating these liabilities included quotes from private firms or government agencies that have worked on the sites, projected planning figures based on related projects, and best engineering judgment.

For contingencies that could arise because of litigation or claims, the Service has certain administrative proceedings, legal actions, and claims pending against it. The Service is involved in three lawsuits in which various plaintiffs are seeking damages estimated at approximately $100 million for alleged "takings" of property rights. The Service has defenses in all three cases and expects to prevail in or settle the pending cases. Any amounts paid by the Government, which are expected to be substantially less than the amounts sought by the plaintiffs, will be paid out of the Judgement Fund of the U.S. Department of the Treasury, rather than from Service appropriations. In the opinion of Service management, as well as the Office of the Solicitor, resolution of these proceedings, actions, and claims will not materially affect the financial position, results of operations, or cash flows of the U.S. Fish and Wildlife Service. Other liabilities not covered by budgetary resources as of September 30, 1999 consist of the following (dollars in thousands):

| | Liabilities Not Covered by Budgetary Resources | |
| --- | --- | --- |
| | Intragovernmental | With the Public |
| Unfunded Payroll Costs | $ 0 | $ 33,435 |
| Actuarial Liabilities | 0 | 38,408 |
| Other Liabilities | 8,825 | 0 |
| Environmental and Contingent Liabilities | 0 | 42,000 |
| Total Other Liabilities Not Covered by Budgetary Resources | $ 8,825 | $ 113,843 |

## NOTE 9. UNEXPENDED APPROPRIATIONS

Unexpended appropriations as of September 30, 1999 (dollars in thousands):

| | Appropriated Funds | Trust Funds | Total |
| --- | --- | --- | --- |
| Unexpended Appropriations | | | |
| Unobligated - Available | $ 295,081 | $ 112,260 | $ 407,341 |
| Unavailable | 11,786 | 0 | 11,786 |
| Undelivered Orders | 400,380 | 285,307 | 685,687 |
| Total Unexpended Appropriations | $ 707,247 | $ 397,567 | $ 1,104,814 |

## NOTE 10.  IMPUTED FINANCING SOURCE

Imputed financing sources are amounts equal to the costs that have been incurred by the reporting entity and budgeted by another entity when services are received at less than full cost.  The Service recognizes the actuarial present value of pensions and other retirement benefits for its employees' during their active years of service.  By recognizing nonbudgetary resources, e.g., the imputed financing source of $32.8 million, the financial statements of the Service reflect the recorded costs that were financed by budgetary resources of the Office of Personnel Management.

## NOTE 11.  PRIOR PERIOD ADJUSTMENTS

The prior period adjustment figure for FY 1999 is comprised of the following (dollars in thousands):

| | | |
|---|---|---:|
| Correct prior period costs that were posted to construction work-in-progress (SGL 1720) which should have been expensed | $ | 73,693 |
| Correct prior period costs originally expensed which should be capitalized assets | | (4,900) |
| Change in capitalized equipment service life | | (868) |
| Correct posting of entries directly to equity | | 14,128 |
| **Total Prior Period Adjustments** | $ | 82,053 |

# United States Department of the Interior

OFFICE OF INSPECTOR GENERAL
Washington, D.C. 20240

AUG - 8 2000

## INDEPENDENT AUDITORS REPORT

Memorandum

To:     Director, U.S. Fish and Wildlife Service

Subject:   Independent Auditors Report on U.S. Fish and Wildlife Service Financial
Statements for Fiscal Year 1999 (No. 00-I-620)

## SUMMARY

In our audit of the U.S. Fish and Wildlife Service's (FWS) financial statements for fiscal
year 1999, we found the following:

- The principal financial statements were fairly presented in all material respects.
FWS's principal financial statements consist of the Balance Sheet as of September 30, 1999
and the Consolidated Statements of Net Cost, Changes in Net Position, Budgetary Resources,
and Financing for the fiscal year ended September 30, 1999.

- Our tests of internal controls identified three material weaknesses related to the
design of internal controls. Specifically, FWS (1) had not designed the interface between
the Federal Finance System (FFS) and the subsidiary Federal aid grants management system
to produce accurate and timely undelivered orders information, (2) did not require Federal
aid grantees to submit documentation to show that grant payments were for costs actually
incurred, and (3) did not have procedures to charge the Construction-in-Progress account
with only FWS real property construction costs and to transfer completed projects out of the
account promptly and into capitalized property or expense accounts as appropriate. FWS
responded to the report on July 5, 2000 (Appendix 1) and generally concurred with the
findings and recommendations to correct the material internal control weaknesses.

- Our tests of compliance with laws and regulations identified no instances of
noncompliance that are required to be reported.

Our conclusions are detailed in the sections that follow.

1

## OPINION ON PRINCIPAL FINANCIAL STATEMENTS

In accordance with the Chief Financial Officers Act of 1990, we audited FWS's principal financial statements for the fiscal year ended September 30, 1999 as contained in FWS's accompanying 1999 Annual Report. These financial statements are the responsibility of FWS, and our responsibility is to express an opinion, based on our audit, on these principal financial statements.

Our audit was conducted in accordance with the "Government Auditing Standards," issued by the Comptroller General of the United States, and with Office of Management and Budget Bulletin 98-08, "Audit Requirements for Federal Financial Statements," as amended. These audit standards require that we plan and perform the audit to obtain reasonable assurance as to whether the accompanying principal financial statements are free of material misstatement. An audit includes examining, on a test basis, evidence supporting the amounts and disclosures contained in the principal financial statements and the accompanying notes. An audit also includes assessing the accounting principles used and the significant estimates made by management. We believe that our audit work provides a reasonable basis for our opinion.

In our opinion, the principal financial statements (pages 40-45) present fairly, in all material respects, the financial position of FWS as of September 30, 1999 and its consolidated net cost, changes in net position, budgetary resources and outlays, and financing for the fiscal year ended September 30, 1999 in conformity with generally accepted accounting principles.

## REPORT ON INTERNAL CONTROLS

Our audit was conducted in accordance with the "Government Auditing Standards," issued by the Comptroller General of the United States, and with Office of Management and Budget Bulletin 98-08.

Management of FWS is responsible for establishing and maintaining an internal control structure which provides reasonable assurance that the following objectives are met:

- Transactions are properly recorded, processed, and summarized to permit the preparation of the principal financial statements and the required supplementary stewardship information in accordance with Federal accounting standards.

- Assets are safeguarded against loss from unauthorized acquisition, use, or disposition.

- Transactions are executed in accordance with (1) laws governing the use of budget authority and with other laws and regulations that could have a direct and material effect on the principal financial statements and the supplemental statements of net cost and changes in net position and (2) any other laws, regulations, and Governmentwide policies identified by the Office of Management and Budget.

2

- Transactions and other data that support reported performance measures are properly recorded, processed, and summarized to permit the preparation of performance information in accordance with criteria stated by management.

Because of inherent limitations in any internal control structure, errors or fraud may occur and not be detected. Also, projections of any evaluation of the internal controls over financial reporting to future periods are subject to the risk that the internal controls may become inadequate because of changes in conditions or that the degree of compliance with the policies or procedures may deteriorate.

In planning and performing our audit, we considered FWS's internal controls over financial reporting by obtaining an understanding of FWS's internal controls, determined whether these internal controls had been placed in operation, assessed control risks, and performed tests of controls in order to determine our auditing procedures for the purpose of expressing an opinion on the principal financial statements and the supplemental statements of net cost and changes in net position and not to provide assurance on the internal controls over financial reporting. Consequently, we do not express an opinion on internal controls.

Our consideration of the internal controls over financial reporting would not necessarily disclose all matters in the internal control structure over financial reporting that might be reportable conditions. Under standards established by the American Institute of Certified Public Accountants and by Office of Management and Budget Bulletin 98-08, reportable conditions are matters coming to our attention relating to significant deficiencies in the design or operation of the internal controls that, in our judgment, could adversely affect FWS's ability to record, process, summarize, and report financial data consistent with the assertions made by management in the principal financial statements. Material weaknesses are reportable conditions in which the design or operation of one or more of the internal control components does not reduce to a relatively low level the risk that misstatements in amounts that would be material in relation to the financial statements being audited may occur and not be detected within a timely period by employees in the normal course of performing their assigned functions. However, we noted matters concerning internal controls and their operation that we consider to be material weaknesses as defined in the preceding sentence. These material weaknesses are described in the paragraphs that follow.

## A. Design of Interface for Federal Aid Undelivered Orders

FWS did not have procedures to accurately and timely update the Undelivered Orders general ledger account related to Federal aid grants to states. Federal Aid Program personnel accounted for the grants to states in a subsidiary system maintained in each FWS regional office and used it to manage the Program. The subsidiary system recorded the original entry for the amount of each new grant and disbursements of grant funds to states based on information from the Department of Health and Human Services Payment Management System on a daily basis. States accessed the Payment Management System for grant disbursements once the FWS regional offices input the grant data into the Payment Management System and authorized the personnel at Health and Human Services to begin

3

the disbursement process. FWS had designed an electronic interface between the Payment Management System and the official financial system (FFS), but the interface did not recognize reductions in undelivered orders resulting from grant closeouts or grant amendments. Additionally, there was a 1-month delay before Payment Management System data updated FFS. This led to additional errors in FFS when regional Program personnel tried to reconcile the subsidiary system with FFS each month because many entries recorded in the subsidiary system had not yet been recorded in FFS. When Program personnel found a missing transaction in FFS, they would initiate manual adjustments to FFS to correct what they perceived to be errors. Later, FFS would be updated with the electronic interface, which resulted in many transactions being duplicated in FFS. To identify and correct the errors, FWS, in October 1999, established a team of finance and Program personnel to reconcile FFS to the subsidiary system. This effort resulted in a net adjustment to decrease the Undelivered Orders account by $23.9 million.

### Recommendation

We recommend that the Director, FWS, redesign the electronic interface between FFS and the Payment Management System to produce accurate and timely information to update the Undelivered Orders general ledger account. Also, the delay in updating FFS with the electronic interface should be eliminated, and written procedures should be developed to reconcile FFS to the subsidiary system. Management should also conduct reviews to ensure that data are accurate.

**FWS Response**: FWS concurred with this finding, stating that it has "completely redesigned" the interface program and that it is "currently being tested." FWS said the new system is scheduled for implementation in July 2000.

### B. Documentation To Support Federal Aid State Grant Costs Incurred

During fiscal year 1999, FWS allowed Federal aid grantees to draw down $424 million on letters of credit for approved grant amounts without requiring all grantees to periodically submit documentation on costs actually incurred. According to the draft Grant Financial System Requirements Manual, published by the Joint Financial Management Improvement Program, an agency's grant financial management system should document the timing of grantees' cash flows, the amounts disbursed to grantees during the year, and the costs actually incurred by the grantees. Although FWS obtained documentation for the approximately 1,300 grants that were closed out during the year, it did not obtain documentation that costs were incurred prior to cash drawdowns for the approximately 3,500 grants that remained open at fiscal year-end. Consequently, FWS could not verify that the payments were for costs incurred or for advances. To provide support for the grant payments on open grants that we sampled, FWS, in a special mailing to grantees, requested grantees to confirm that the drawdowns were for costs actually incurred. The grantees verified that the drawdowns were for costs incurred.

4

## Recommendation

We recommend that the Director, FWS, develop and implement procedures for the Federal Aid Program to validate, for financial reporting purposes, that costs were incurred by all grantees prior to drawing down cash.

**FWS Response:** FWS did not agree with this recommendation, stating that it has controls to ensure that grantees withdraw funds only for costs incurred previously. FWS further said that its controls included "[m]onthly reconciliations of withdrawals with documentation of costs incurred provided to Service officials." FWS also said that the system "as a whole provides reasonable assurance that the drawdowns are for costs incurred" and that it planned to "consider additional steps to increase assurance that grantees drawdowns are for costs incurred." FWS further said it would consider the feasibility of sampling a limited number of FY [fiscal year] 2000 drawdowns to verify that "withdrawals were for costs incurred."

**OIG Reply.** We believe that as part of FWS's financial records, documentation of the fact that disbursements were used only for costs previously incurred is essential, and the actions proposed by FWS meet the intent of this recommendation.

## C. Procedures To Ensure Accurate Construction in Progress

The Construction-in-Progress general ledger account was overstated by $114.5 million. The account was used to accumulate building and structure construction project costs that had not been completed as of the date of the financial statements. The overstatement occurred because FWS did not have procedures to ensure that charges to the account were reviewed promptly and that the charges were for FWS's building and structure assets (real property) that would meet FWS's $50,000 capitalization threshold. As a result, the account contained costs of $13.8 million that were for completed projects that had not been moved to real property accounts or that had not been expensed as appropriate; costs of $17.9 million that were for misclassified operations, maintenance, and expendable property costs; and costs of $82.8 million that were not for real property, such as hazardous waste cleanup costs. On December 15, 1999, FWS issued additional real property reconciliation procedures that addressed these issues.

## Recommendation

We recommend that the Director, FWS, ensure that the additional real property procedures are implemented as designed.

**FWS Response:** FWS stated that it had designed and implemented the real property reconciliation procedures in December 1999.

5

## STEWARDSHIP AND PERFORMANCE MEASURES

We considered FWS's internal controls over the required supplementary stewardship information (pages 23-35) by obtaining an understanding of FWS's internal controls relating to the preparation of the required supplementary stewardship information to determine whether these internal controls had been placed in operation and performed tests of these controls as required by Bulletin 98-08. However, providing assurance on these internal controls was not an objective of our audit, and accordingly, we do not provide assurance on such controls.

With respect to the internal controls related to the performance measures reported in FWS's program highlights (pages 1-21), we obtained an understanding of the design of significant internal controls related to the existence and completeness assertions as required by Bulletin No. 98-08. Our procedures were not designed to provide assurance on internal controls over reported performance measures, and accordingly, we do not provide an opinion on such controls.

## REPORT ON COMPLIANCE WITH LAWS AND REGULATIONS

Our audit was conducted in accordance with the "Government Auditing Standards," issued by the Comptroller General of the United States, and with Office of Management and Budget Bulletin 98-08.

Management of FWS is responsible for complying with laws and regulations applicable to that agency. As part of obtaining reasonable assurance about whether FWS's principal financial statements are free of material misstatement, we performed tests of FWS's compliance with certain provisions of laws and regulations, noncompliance with which could have a direct and material effect on the determination of financial statements amounts and certain other laws and regulations specified in Bulletin 98-08, including the requirements referred to in the Federal Financial Management Improvement Act of 1996. However, providing an opinion on compliance with certain provisions of laws and regulations was not an objective of our audit, and accordingly, we do not express such an opinion.

The results of our tests of compliance with laws and regulations discussed in the preceding paragraph exclusive of the Federal Financial Management Improvement Act disclosed no instances of noncompliance that are required to be reported under the "Government Auditing Standards" or Bulletin 98-08.

Under the Federal Financial Management Improvement Act, we are required to report whether FWS's financial management systems were in substantial compliance with requirements for Federal financial management systems, Federal accounting standards, and the U.S. Government Standard General Ledger at the transaction level. To meet these requirements, we performed tests of compliance using the implementation guidance for the Federal Financial Management Improvement Act included in Appendix D of Bulletin 98-08.

6

The results of our tests disclosed no instances in which FWS's financial management system was not in substantial compliance with these three requirements.

## CONSISTENCY OF OTHER INFORMATION

We reviewed the financial information presented in FWS's program highlights (pages 1-21) and supplementary information (pages 23-35) to determine whether the information was consistent with the principal financial statements. Based on our review, we determined that the information in the overview was consistent with the principal financial statements.

## PRIOR AUDIT COVERAGE

We reviewed prior Office of Inspector General and General Accounting Office audit reports related to FWS's financial statements to determine whether these reports contained any unresolved or unimplemented recommendations that were significant to FWS's financial statements or internal controls. We found that there were no reports issued by the Office of Inspector General that contained significant unresolved or unimplemented recommendations related to FWS's financial statements or internal controls. The General Accounting Office, however, issued, in February 2000, the letter "Financial Management Review of the U.S. Fish and Wildlife Service's Reported Allocation of Resources for its Refuge Program and New Assistant Regional Manager Positions." The letter stated that FWS did not use its accounting system to track the costs of the refuge program on a full-cost basis, as required by Department of the Interior policy and Statement of Federal Financial Accounting Standards No. 4, "Managerial Cost Accounting Standards." The General Accounting Office recommended that FWS identify and accumulate direct and indirect costs, distribute indirect costs, and monitor and evaluate the full cost of its outputs. FWS agreed with and, at the time of our review, was implementing the recommendation as it related to its three mission goals but not as it related to its refuge program.

## OBJECTIVE, SCOPE, AND METHODOLOGY

Management of FWS is responsible for the following:

- Preparing the principal financial statements and the required supplemental information referred to in the Consistency of Other Information section of this report in conformity with generally accepted accounting principles and for preparing the other information contained in the 1999 Annual Report.

- Establishing and maintaining an internal control structure over financial reporting. In fulfilling this responsibility, estimates and judgments are required to assess the expected benefits and related costs of internal control structure policies and procedures.

- Complying with applicable laws and regulations.

We are responsible for the following:

7

- Expressing an opinion on FWS's principal financial statements.

- Obtaining an understanding regarding the effectiveness of the internal controls based upon the internal control objectives contained in Bulletin 98-08, which require that transactions be properly recorded, processed, and summarized to permit the preparation of the principal financial statements and the required supplemental information in accordance with Federal accounting standards; that assets be safeguarded against loss from unauthorized acquisition, use, or disposal; and that transactions and other data that support reported performance measures be properly recorded, processed, and summarized to permit the preparation of performance information in accordance with criteria stated by management.

- Testing FWS's compliance with selected provisions of laws and regulations that could materially affect the principal financial statements or the required supplementary information.

To fulfill these responsibilities, we took the following actions:

- Examined, on a test basis, evidence supporting the amounts disclosed in the principal financial statements.

- Assessed the accounting principles used and the significant estimates made by management.

- Evaluated the overall presentation of the financial statements.

- Obtained an understanding of the internal control structure related to safeguarding of assets; compliance with laws and regulations, including the execution of transactions in accordance with budget authority; financial reporting; and certain performance measure information reported in the Program Highlights.

- Tested relevant internal controls over the safeguarding of assets; compliance with laws and regulations, including the execution of transactions in accordance with budget authority; and financial reporting.

- Reviewed the internal controls relevant to the existence and completeness assertions for systems producing the performance measures reported in the Program Highlights.

- Tested compliance with selected provisions of laws and regulations.

We did not evaluate all of the internal controls related to the operating objectives as broadly defined in the Federal Managers' Financial Integrity Act, such as those controls related to preparing statistical reports and ensuring efficient operations. We limited our internal control testing to those controls necessary to achieve the objectives outlined in our report on internal controls.

8

We also identified other issues that, in our judgment, were not required to be included in this audit report but that should be communicated to management. We have included these issues in a management letter that was issued separately.

Based on FWS's July 5, 2000, response, we consider Recommendations A.1, B.1, and C.1 resolved and implemented.

Since the recommendations are considered resolved and implemented, no further response to this report is required (see Appendix 2).

Section 5(a) of the Inspector General Act (5 U.S.C. app. 3) requires the Office of Inspector General to list this report in its semiannual report to the Congress. In addition, the Office of Inspector General provides audit reports to the Congress.

This report is intended for the information of management of FWS and the Office of Management and Budget and the Congress. However, this report is a matter of public record, and its distribution is not limited.

Roger La Rouche
Acting Assistant Inspector General
for Audits

9

# United States Department of the Interior

FISH AND WILDLIFE SERVICE
Washington, D.C. 20240

IN REPLY REFER TO:

FWS/DF

Memorandum

To:       Assistant Inspector General for Audits
Office of Inspector General
(Attn: Director of Financial Audits)

From:     Director                 JUL 5 2000

Subject:   Comments on Draft Auditor's Report on U.S. Fish and Wildlife Service Financial
Statements for Fiscal Year 1999

After reviewing the draft audit report, the Service generally concurs with the findings and
recommendations regarding the three identified internal control matters. Presented below are the
actions taken or planned to address each identified issue:

Design of Interface for Federal Aid Undelivered Orders

We agree that the interface between the Department of Health and Human Service's Payment
Management System and the Service's Federal Financial System in operation in FY 1999 required
improvement, and that as a result, considerable effort was required to ensure that the information on
Federal Aid undelivered orders contained in Service accounting records was accurate. The interface
program has been completely redesigned and is currently being tested. It is scheduled for
implementation in July 2000.

Documentation To Support Federal Aid State Grant Costs Incurred

We do not believe it is appropriate, feasible, or required by statute or regulation to acquire
documentation for 3500 Federal Aid grants to validate that costs were incurred prior to cash
drawdowns. Such an approach would be time consuming and labor intensive, and would not
significantly alter the risk that some cash may be incorrectly reported as reimbursements. Such a risk
is already very low. Our approach is to increase the Service's assurance that drawdowns are for costs
incurred without increasing the costs of administering the Federal Aid program or unnecessarily
burdening grant recipients. To date there is no evidence to suggest that any grantee intentionally
withdrew funds prior to incurring costs, or that systemic problems with cash advances exist.

There are numerous controls currently in place to ensure that grantees only withdraw funds for
previously incurred costs. These controls include:

10

- Language in the Service Manual chapter on Federal Aid Program Standards for Administration that specifically states that payments to grantees are for costs incurred
- Defense Contract Audit Agency audits of Federal Aid grants that specifically address whether funds are withdrawn by grantees prior to incurring costs
- Monthly reconciliations of withdrawals with documentation of costs incurred provided to Service officials

As noted in the audit report, the Service also sampled more than 80 FY 1999 open grants and received confirmation from all grantees (except the State of Tennessee which did not respond) that their drawdowns were for costs incurred. We also received attestations from Federal Aid program managers that the withdrawals by grantees were cost reimbursements. We recognize these measures do not validate that all withdrawals were for incurred costs. However we believe that the system, taken as a whole, provides reasonable assurance that drawdowns are for costs incurred.

We plan to consider additional steps to provide increased assurance that grantees drawdowns are for costs incurred, including:

- Adding specific language to the list of assurances provided by grantees reiterating that drawdowns are only for costs already incurred
- Issuing a policy statement to grantees that payments are for incurred expenses
- Requiring financial status reports at the end of each fiscal year for all open grants.

We will also consider the feasibility of sampling a limited number of FY 2000 drawdowns to verify that State withdrawals were for costs incurred.

Procedures to Ensure Accurate Construction in Progress

The report recognizes that in December 1999, the Service designed and implemented real property reconciliation procedures that addressed the reported overstatement error. As a result of the improvements made to the reconciliation procedures, the Service considers this issue to be resolved. However, we understand that the Office of Inspector General needs to review and monitor implementing actions conducted by the Service in FY 2000 to verify that this issue has been corrected. We will continue to work with the Office of Inspector General in its review of periodic data and supporting documentation. The data related to Construction in Progress accounts is incorporated into the Service's financial statement presentation and is available through the Hyperion financial application. The Service can provide supporting documentation of the data recorded in Hyperion, as requested.

We believe that the actions stated above accomplish the intent of the report's recommendations. If you have any questions or need more information, please contact Dave Holland, Chief, Division of Finance, at (703) 358-1742.

cc:  Mr. Keith Clark, Senior Auditor, OIG

11

- Language in the Service Manual chapter on Federal Aid Program Standards for Administration that specifically states that payments to grantees are for costs incurred
- Defense Contract Audit Agency audits of Federal Aid grants that specifically address whether funds are withdrawn by grantees prior to incurring costs
- Monthly reconciliations of withdrawals with documentation of costs incurred provided to Service officials

As noted in the audit report, the Service also sampled more than 80 FY 1999 open grants and received confirmation from all grantees (except the State of Tennessee which did not respond) that their drawdowns were for costs incurred. We also received attestations from Federal Aid program managers that the withdrawals by grantees were cost reimbursements. We recognize these measures do not validate that all withdrawals were for incurred costs. However we believe that the system, taken as a whole, provides reasonable assurance that drawdowns are for costs incurred.

We plan to consider additional steps to provide increased assurance that grantees drawdowns are for costs incurred, including:

- Adding specific language to the list of assurances provided by grantees reiterating that drawdowns are only for costs already incurred
- Issuing a policy statement to grantees that payments are for incurred expenses
- Requiring financial status reports at the end of each fiscal year for all open grants.

We will also consider the feasibility of sampling a limited number of FY 2000 drawdowns to verify that State withdrawals were for costs incurred.

Procedures to Ensure Accurate Construction in Progress

The report recognizes that in December 1999, the Service designed and implemented real property reconciliation procedures that addressed the reported overstatement error. As a result of the improvements made to the reconciliation procedures, the Service considers this issue to be resolved. However, we understand that the Office of Inspector General needs to review and monitor implementing actions conducted by the Service in FY 2000 to verify that this issue has been corrected. We will continue to work with the Office of Inspector General in its review of periodic data and supporting documentation. The data related to Construction in Progress accounts is incorporated into the Service's financial statement presentation and is available through the Hyperion financial application. The Service can provide supporting documentation of the data recorded in Hyperion, as requested.

We believe that the actions stated above accomplish the intent of the report's recommendations. If you have any questions or need more information, please contact Dave Holland, Chief, Division of Finance, at (703) 358-1742.


cc:   Mr. Keith Clark, Senior Auditor, OIG

11

## STATUS OF AUDIT REPORT RECOMMENDATIONS

| Finding/Recommendation Reference | Status | Action Required |
|---|---|---|
| A.1, B.1 and C.1 | Implemented. | No further action is required. |

12

# Supplemental Information

The U.S. Department of the Interior

U.S. Fish and Wildlife Service

Regional Offices

**Region 1**

U.S. Fish and Wildlife Service
911 N.E. 11th Avenue
Portland, OR 97232-4181
*(CA, HI, ID, NV, OR, WA,*
*Trust Territories of the Pacific)*

**Region 2**

U.S. Fish and Wildlife Service
500 Gold Avenue
P.O. Box 1306
Albuquerque, NM 87103
*(AZ, NM, OK, TX)*

**Region 3**

U.S. Fish and Wildlife Service
One Federal Drive
Fort Snelling, MN 55111-4056
*(IA, IL, IN, MI, MN, MO, OH,*
*WI)*

**Region 4**

U.S. Fish and Wildlife Service
1875 Century Boulevard
Atlanta, GA 30345
*(AL, AR, FL, GA, KY, LA, MS,*
*NC, PR, SC, TN, VI)*

**Region 5**

U.S. Fish and Wildlife Service
300 Westgate Center Drive
Hadley, MA 01035-9589
*(CT, DC, DE, MA, MD, ME, NH,*
*NJ, NY, PA, RI, VA, VT, WV)*

**Region 6**

U.S. Fish and Wildlife Service
P.O. Box 25486
Denver Federal Center
Denver, CO 80225
*(CO, KS, MT, ND, NE, SD, UT,*
*WY)*

**Region 7**

U.S. Fish and Wildlife Service
1011 Tudor Road
Anchorage, AK 99503
*(AK)*

**Headquarters**

U.S. Fish and Wildlife Service
4401 N. Fairfax Drive
Arlington, VA 22203

If you have any comments or suggestions, please write to:

U.S. Fish and Wildlife Service

Division of Finance

4401 N. Fairfax Drive

Suite 380

Arlington, Virginia 22203

To find information about all aspects of the

U.S. Fish and Wildlife Service, explore our web site at:

http://www.fws.gov

Inside Cover Photo Credit: USFWS/Larry Aumiller

U.S. Department of the Interior
U.S. Fish & Wildlife Service
http://www.fws.gov

August 2000

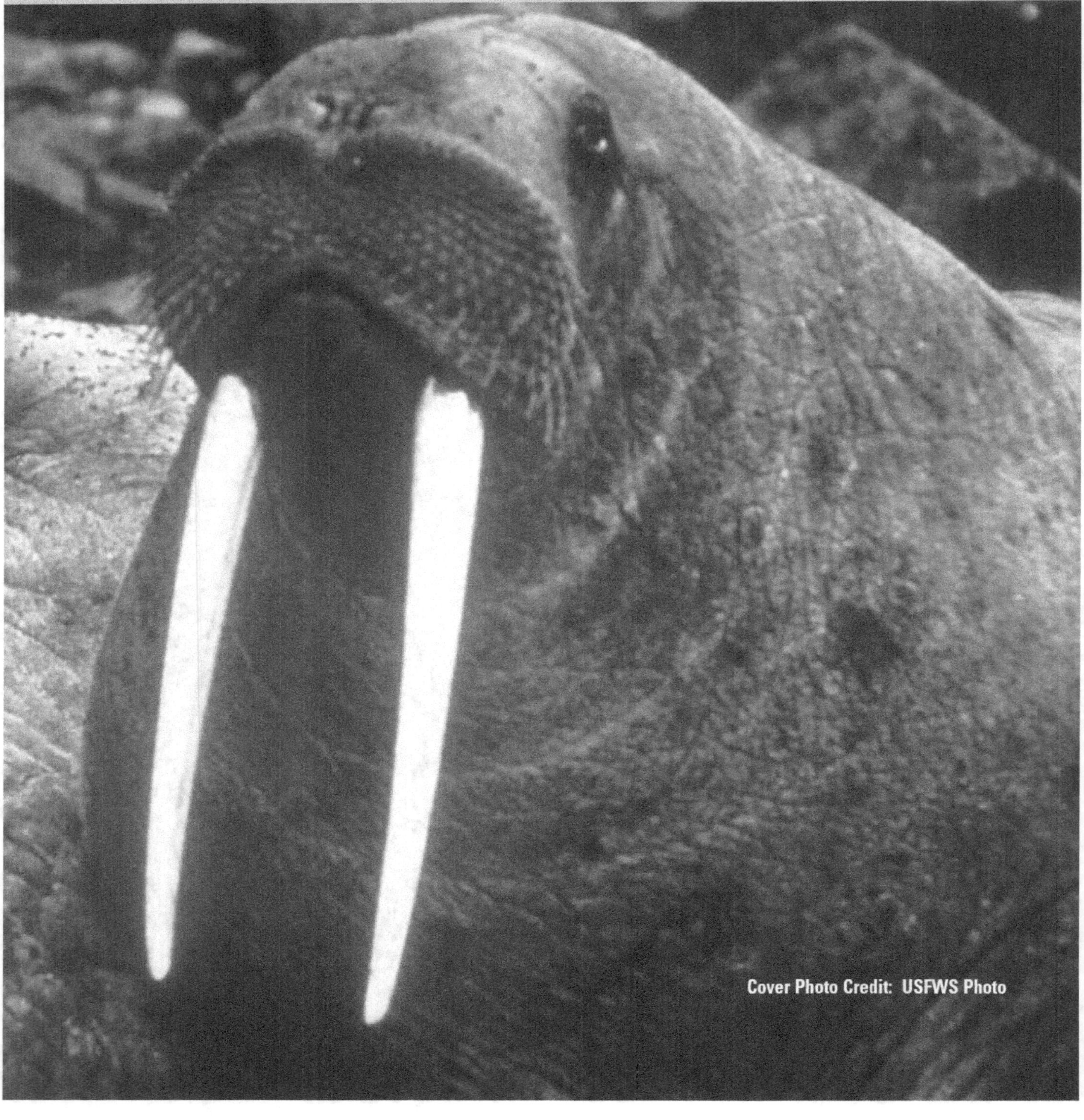